DB2 9 for Linux, UNIX, and Windows
Database Administration Upgrade
Certification Study Guide

DB2 9

for Linux, UNIX, and Windows

Database Administration Upgrade

Certification Study Guide

Roger E. Sanders

MC PRESS

MC Press Online, LP
Lewisville, TX 75077

DB2 9 for Linux, UNIX, and Windows Database Administration Upgrade Certification Study Guide
Roger E. Sanders

First Edition

First Printing—October 2007

© 2007 Roger Sanders. All rights reserved.

MC Press offers excellent discounts on this book when ordered in quantity for bulk purchases or special sales, which may include custom covers and content particular to your business, training goals, marketing focus, and branding interest.

For information regarding permissions or special orders, please contact:
    MC Press
    Corporate Offices
    125 N. Woodland Trail
    Lewisville, TX 75077 USA

For information regarding sales and/or customer service, please contact:
    MC Press
    P.O. Box 4300
    Big Sandy, TX 75755-4300 USA

ISBN 10: 158347-078-6
ISBN 13: 978-158347-078-7

Dedication

To my sister, Kathy

Acknowledgments

A project of this magnitude requires both a great deal of time and the support of many different individuals. I would like to express my gratitude to the following people for their contributions:

Susan Dykman – Information Management Certification Program Manager, IBM Information Management
Susan invited me to participate in the DB2 9 exam development process, and provided me with screen shots of the IBM Certification Exam Testing software. Susan also reviewed the first chapter of the book and provided valuable feedback.

Susan Visser – IBM Press, Data Management Program Manager
IBM Toronto Lab
Once again, Susan's help was invaluable; without her help, this book would not have been written. Susan paved the way for me to acquire the rights to the Version 8.1 manuscript and move to MC Press when Pearson Education decided not to publish an updated version of my Version 8.1 book. Susan also reviewed many of the chapters as they were written, and she made sure the appropriate subject-matter experts at the IBM Toronto Lab reviewed portions of the manuscript as well.

Dr. Arvind Krishna – Vice President, IBM Data Servers and Worldwide Information Management Development
Dr. Krishna provided me with the Foreword for this book.

Reed M. Meseck – Senior Competitive Specialist, IBM Information Management Software
Reed helped Dr. Arvind Krishna develop the Foreword for this book.

Brant Davison – Program Director, IBM Information Management Software
Brant worked with me to ensure that Dr. Arvind Krishna received the materials he needed to develop the Foreword for this book.

Jason Gartner – Executive Assistant to Arvind Krishna
Jason worked with Reed Meseck and Dr. Arvind Krishna to make sure I received the Foreword for this book in a timely manner.

Rick Swagerman – Sr. Technical Manager, DB2 SQL and Catalog Development IBM Toronto Lab

Rick provided me with detailed examples illustrating how the UPDATE/DELETE NO ACTION and UPDATE/DELETE RESTRICT rules of referential constraints work. His examples were converted into some of the illustrations you see in Chapter 4, and Rick reviewed the final draft of many of these drawings for accuracy and completeness.

Dale McInnis – Sr. Technical Staff Member, DB2 High Availability IBM Toronto Lab

Dale reviewed the material in Chapter 7 – High Availability for accuracy and completeness; the valuable feedback he provided was I incorporated into the chapter.

I would also like to thank my wife Beth for her help and encouragement, and for once again overlooking all of the things that did not get done while I worked on yet another (my 16th) book.

About the Author

Roger E. Sanders is the President of Roger Sanders Enterprises, Inc. He has been designing and developing database applications for more than 20 years and has been working with DB2 and its predecessors since it was first introduced on the IBM PC (as part of OS/2 Extended Edition). He has written articles for publications such as *Certification Magazine* and *IDUG Solutions Journal*, authored tutorials for IBM's developerWorks Web site, presented at numerous International DB2 User's Group (IDUG) and Regional DB2 User's Group (RUG) conferences, taught classes on DB2 fundamentals and database administration (DB2 for Linux, UNIX, and Windows), writes a regular column called *Distributed DBA* in DB2 Magazine, and is the author of the following books:

- *DB2 9 for Linux, UNIX, and Windows Database Administration Certification Exam Study Guide*

- *Using the IBM System Storage N Series with Databases* (IBM RedBook; co-author)

- *DB2 9 Fundamentals Certification Study Guide*

- *Integrating IBM DB2 with the IBM System Storage N Series* (IBM RedBook; co-author)

- *Using IBM DB2UDB with IBM System Storage N Series* (IBM RedBook; co-author)

- *DB2 Universal Database V8.1 Certification Exam 703 Study Guide*

- *DB2 Universal Database V8.1 Certification Exam 701 and 706 Study Guide*

- *DB2 Universal Database V8.1 Certification Exam 700 Study Guide*

- *DB2 UDB Exploitation of NAS Technology* (IBM RedBook; co-author)

- *All-In-One DB2 Administration Exam Guide*

- *DB2 Universal Database SQL Developer's Guide*

- *DB2 Universal Database API Developer's Guide*

- *DB2 Universal Database Call Level Interface Developer's Guide*

- *ODBC 3.5 Developer's Guide*

- *The Developer's Handbook to DB2 for Common Servers*

In addition, Roger holds the following professional certifications:

- IBM Certified Advanced Database Administrator—DB2 9 for Linux, UNIX, and Windows

- IBM Certified Application Developer—DB2 9

- IBM Certified Database Administrator—DB2 9 DBA for Linux, UNIX, and Windows

- IBM Certified Database Associate—DB2 9 Fundamentals

- IBM Certified Advanced Database Administrator—DB2 Universal Database V8.1 for Linux, UNIX, and Windows

- IBM Certified Database Administrator—DB2 Universal Database V8.1 for Linux, UNIX, and Windows

- IBM Certified Developer—DB2 Universal Database V8.1 Family

- IBM Certified Database Associate—DB2 Universal Database V8.1 Family

- IBM Certified Advanced Technical Expert—DB2 for Clusters

- IBM Certified Solutions Expert—DB2 UDB V7.1 Database Administration for UNIX, Windows, and OS/2

- IBM Certified Solutions Expert—DB2 UDB V6.1 Application Development for UNIX, Windows, and OS/2

- IBM Certified Specialist—DB2 UDB V6/V7 User

About This Book

This book is divided into two parts:

- Part 1 – DB2 UDB Certification (Chapter 1)

  This section consists of one chapter (Chapter 1), which is designed to introduce you to the DB2 Professional Certification Program that is available from IBM. In this chapter, you will learn about the *IBM Certified Database Administrator – DB2 9 for Linux, UNIX, and Windows* certification role and you will be presented with the objectives that have been developed for the DB2 9 for Linux, UNIX, and Windows Database Administration Upgrade exam (Exam 736). This chapter also explains what's involved in the certification process.

- Part 2 – DB2 9 Database Administration Concepts (Chapters 2–7)

  This section consists of six chapters (Chapters 2 through 7), which are designed to provide you with the concepts you will need to master before you can pass the DB2 9 for Linux, UNIX, and Windows Database Administration Upgrade exam (Exam 736).

  Chapter 2 is designed to introduce you to the various aspects of server management. In this chapter, you will learn how to use the Configuration Advisor to configure servers, instances, and databases, as well as how to configure client communications. You will also learn how to configure a database for Automatic Maintenance, how to use the Self-Tuning Memory Manager, and how to throttle utilities to control their impact on database workloads.

  Chapter 3 is designed to teach you everything you need to know about how data in a DB2 9 database is physically stored. In this chapter, you will learn how to create a DB2 9 database and you will discover what a DB2 9 database's underlying structure looks like, as well as how that structure is mapped to files and directories. You will also learn how to create Automatic Storage table spaces, how to partition data with table (range) partitioning, and how to configure a table to use data row compression.

Chapter 4 is designed to provide you with information about creating databases and tables that support XML. In this chapter, you will learn how to enable a database for XML data storage, how to use the XML data type, how to manipulate XML data and create XML indexes, how to use basic XML functions, and how to process XML data when using DB2's data movement utilities.

Chapter 5 is designed to introduce you to the various tools that are available for monitoring a database's performance. In this chapter, you will learn how to configure and use the snapshot monitor and how to create one or more event monitors. You will also learn how to use the DB2 Problem Determination Tool – db2pd.

Chapter 6 is designed to introduce you to the concept of database backup and recovery and to the various tools available with DB2 9 that can be used to return a damaged or corrupted database to a useable and consistent state. In this chapter, you will learn what transaction logging is, how transaction logging is performed, and how log files are used to restore a damaged database. You will learn how to make backup images of a database or a table space using the Backup utility, how to perform version recovery using the Restore utility, how to reapply transaction records stored in logs to perform a roll forward recovery operation using the Roll-forward utility, and how to restore a database using information stored in the recovery history log file using the Recover utility. You will also learn how to set up a High Availability Disaster Recovery (HADR) environment.

Chapter 7 is designed to introduce you to the concept of database security and to the various authorization levels and privileges that are recognized by DB2. In this chapter, you will learn how and where users are authenticated, how authorities and privileges determine what a user can and cannot do while working with a database, and how authorities and privileges are given to and taken away from individual users and/or groups of individual users. You will also learn how to restrict access to specific columns and/or rows in a table using Label-Based Access Control (LBAC).

The book is written primarily for IT professionals who have a great deal of experience working with DB2 9, already hold the IBM Certified Database Administrator—DB2 V8.1 for Linux, UNIX, and Windows certification, and would like to take (and pass) the DB2 9 for Linux, UNIX, and Windows Database Administration Upgrade exam (Exam 736).

Conventions Used

Many examples of DB2 9 administrative commands and SQL statements can be found throughout this book. The following conventions are used whenever a DB2 command or SQL statement is presented:

[ ]   Parameters or items shown inside of brackets are required and must be provided.

< >   Parameters or items shown inside of angle brackets are optional and do not have to be provided.

| Vertical bars are used to indicate that one (and only one) item in the list of items presented can be specified

,...   A comma followed by three periods (ellipsis) indicate that multiple instances of the preceding parameter or item can be included in the DB2 command or SQL statement

The following examples illustrate each of these conventions:

Example 1

```
REFRESH TABLE [TableName ,...]
<INCREMENTAL | NON INCREMENTAL>
```

In this example, at least one *TableName* value must be provided, as indicated by the brackets ([ ]), and more than one *TableName* value can be provided, as indicated by the comma-ellipsis (, . . .) characters that follow the *TableName* parameter. INCREMENTAL and NON INCREMENTAL are optional, as indicated by the angle brackets (< >), and either one or the other can be specified, but not both, as indicated by the vertical bar (|).

Example 2

```
CREATE SEQUENCE [SequenceName]
<AS [SMALLINT | INTEGER | BIGINT | DECIMAL]>
<START WITH [StartingNumber]>
<INCREMENT BY [1 | Increment]>
<NO MINVALUE | MINVALUE [MinValue]>
<NO MAXVALUE | MAXVALUE [MaxValue]>
<NO CYCLE | CYCLE>
<NO CACHE | CACHE 20 | CACHE [CacheValue]>
<NO ORDER | ORDER>
```

In this example, a *SequenceName* value must be provided, as indicated by the brackets ([ ]). However, everything else is optional, as indicated by the angle brackets (< >), and in many cases, a list of available option values is provided (for example, NO CYCLE and CYCLE); however, only one can be specified, as indicated by the vertical bar (|). In addition, when some options are provided (for example, START WITH, INCREMENT BY, MINVALUE, MAXVALUE, and CACHE), a corresponding value must be provided, as indicated by the brackets ([ ]) that follow the option.

SQL is not a case-sensitive language, but for clarity, the examples provided are shown in mixed case—command syntax is presented in uppercase while user-supplied elements such as table names and column names are presented in lower case. However, the examples shown can be entered in any case.

Although basic syntax is presented for most of the DB2 commands and SQL statements covered in this book, the actual syntax supported may be much more complex. To view the complete syntax for a specific command or to obtain more information about a particular command, refer to the *IBM DB2, Version 9 Command Reference* product documentation. To view the complete syntax for a specific SQL statement or to obtain more information about a particular statement, refer to the *IBM DB2, Version 9 SQL Reference, Volume 2* product documentation.

Contents

Foreword

We live in a world of information. But how did we get here? We started with the goal of reaching the moon, and conquering the task of moving data between a tiny spacecraft and the earth, and then storing that data in a reliable and quickly accessible way.

We developed new technologies, new systems, and new software to transmit, process, and store that data. Today, we live in an era where processing power continues to soar, and where the sky is the limit for storage capacity. The result has been an unprecedented flood of data.

Today, the goal is not just storing data, but providing ubiquitous access to information. We live in a world of information, and increasingly we expect our world to be an On Demand world: always on, always available, where information is increasingly rich and dynamic, immediate and instantaneous.

We access information with our laptops, our cell phones, our Blackberrys—at our desks and on the road. Increasingly your success is dependent upon your ability to easily access and connect that information across the organization and across the globe.

IBM's goal is to help our customers and partners transform from data and information management to Information On Demand. Information On Demand is about getting the right information to the right people, at the right time, in the right context.

Today, the greatest competitive advantages are often gained from uncovering data you already have and connecting it easily, seamlessly and ubiquitously: Information as a Service. Only IBM has the vision and the breadth of products and services to make this vision a reality and DB2 is the Data Server for your On Demand world.

Data servers are a critical element of your IT foundation, and DB2 is the Data Server of choice for customers running a broad spectrum of applications, from On-Line Transaction Processing to Data Warehousing, from Web Services to Analytics, from small to extreme data volume. From the no-charge DB2

Express-C to advanced capabilities for transactional and dynamic warehousing applications, IBM offers the right data server for the job.

Today, DB2 runs in the top 25 banks worldwide, 23 of the top 25 U.S. retailers, and 9 of the top 10 global life and health insurance providers. DB2 is the choice of a growing number of ISVs and customers running ISV applications such as SAP. Last year alone, over 4,500 new customers chose DB2 to run their businesses. And with the delivery of DB2 9, we are seeing that growth accelerate. We now have over 450,000 customers using IBM Data Servers to run their businesses across industries and across the globe.

DB2 is the only data server that consistently delivers leading performance in TPC-C, TPC-H and SAP application benchmarks. But more importantly, DB2 continues to deliver reliability and security for your business and applications.

DB2 9 provides another proof point of what makes IBM different-from the invention of database technology in 1966 to support the Apollo space program; to the invention of the relational data model in the 70s; to the 68 patented innovations in DB2 9, to the more than 3,000 data management patents—IBM continues to lead in innovations that help our clients deliver business results.

Information is the fabric of global businesses, and data server professionals will continue to be critical to the delivery, management, and governance of this corporate asset. Roger Sanders has provided a tremendous opportunity to learn more about DB2, and I encourage you to take advantage this opportunity and learn skills you can leverage to deliver more value to your business. Your time spent will be valuable to you and your colleagues.

Arvind Krishna
IBM Corporation
Vice President
Data Servers and Information Management Development

Preface

One of the biggest challenges computer professionals face today is keeping their skill sets current with the latest changes in technology. When the computing industry was in its infancy, it was possible to become an expert in several different areas, because the scope of the field was relatively small. Today, our industry is both widespread and fast paced, and the skills needed to master a single software package can be quite complex. Because of this complexity, many application and hardware vendors have initiated certification programs to evaluate and validate an individual's knowledge of their technology. Businesses benefit from these programs, because professional certification gives them confidence that an individual has the expertise needed to perform a specific job. Computer professionals benefit, because professional certification allows them to deliver high levels of service and technical expertise, and more importantly, professional certification can lead to advancement and/or new job opportunities within the computer industry.

If you've bought this book (or if you are thinking about buying this book), chances are you have already decided you want to acquire one or more of the IBM DB2 professional certifications available. As an individual who holds twelve IBM DB2 professional certifications, let me assure you that the exams you must pass in order to become a certified DB2 professional are not easy. IBM prides itself on designing comprehensive certification exams that are relevant to the work environment to which an individual holding a particular certification will be exposed. As a result, all of IBM's certification exams are designed with the following items in mind:

- What are the critical tasks that must be performed by an individual who holds a particular professional certification?

- What skills must an individual possess in order to perform each critical task identified?

- How frequently will an individual perform each critical task identified?

You will find that to pass a DB2 certification exam, you must possess a solid understanding of DB2. For some of the more advanced certifications, you must understand many of the DB2 nuances as well.

Now for the good news. You are holding in your hands what I consider to be the best tool you can use to prepare for the DB2 9 for Linux, UNIX, and Windows Database Administration Upgrade exam (Exam 736). When IBM began work on the DB2 9 certification exams, I was invited once again to participate in the exam development process. In addition to helping define the exam objectives, I authored several exam questions and I provided feedback on many more before the final exams went into production. Consequently, I have seen every exam question you are likely to encounter, and I know every concept on which you will be tested when you take the DB2 9 for Linux, UNIX, and Windows Database Administration Ugrade exam (Exam 736). Using this knowledge, along with copies of the actual exam questions, I developed this study guide, which not only covers every concept you must know in order to pass the DB2 9 for Linux, UNIX, and Windows Database Administration Upgrade exam (Exam 736), but also covers the exam process itself and the requirements for each DB2 9 certification role available. In addition, you will find at the end of each chapter, the sample questions that are worded just like the actual exam questions. In short, if you see it in this book, count on seeing it on the exam; if you don't see it in this book, it won't be on the exam. If you become familiar with the material presented in this book, you should do well on the exam.

IBM DB2 9 Certification

Recognized throughout the world, the Professional Certification Program from IBM offers a range of certification options for IT professionals. This program consists of several distinct certification roles that are designed to guide you in your professional development; you begin the certification process by selecting the role that's right for you, and familiarizing yourself with the certification requirements for that role. Once you have chosen the certification role you wish to pursue and have familiarized yourself with the requirements for that particular role, the next step is to prepare for and take the appropriate certification exam or exams.

This chapter is designed to introduce you to an accelerated path you can take to obtain the *IBM Certified Database Administrator – DB2 9 for Linux, UNIX, and Windows* certification from IBM.

IBM Certified Database Administrator – DB2 9 for Linux, UNIX, and Windows

The *IBM Certified Database Administrator – DB2 9 for Linux, UNIX, and Windows* certification is intended for experienced DB2 9 users who possess the knowledge and skills necessary to perform the day-to-day administration of DB2 9 instances and databases residing on Linux, UNIX, or Windows platforms. In addition to being knowledgeable about the concepts of DB2 9 database administration, individuals seeking this certification should have significant hands-on experience as a DB2 9 Database Administrator (DBA).

Candidates who have either taken and passed the **DB2 V8.1 Family Fundamentals** exam (Exam 700) or acquired the IBM Certified Database Administrator – DB2 V8.1 for Linux, UNIX, and Windows certification (by taking and passing Exams 700 and 701) must take and pass the **DB2 9 for Linux, UNIX, and Windows Database Administration** exam (Exam 731) to acquire the IBM Certified Database Administrator—DB2 9 for Linux, UNIX, and Windows certification. All other candidates must take and pass both the **DB2 9 Family Fundamentals** exam (Exam 730) and the **DB2 9 for Linux, UNIX, and Windows Database Administration** exam (Exam 731). The roadmap for acquiring the IBM Certified Database Administrator – DB2 9 for Linux, UNIX, and Windows certification can be seen in Figure 1–1.

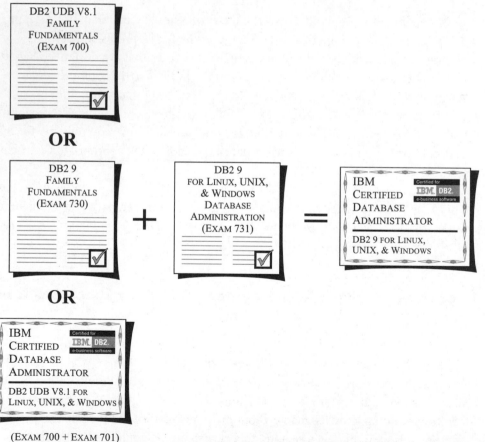

Figure 1–1: IBM Certified Database Administrator – DB2 9 for Linux, UNIX, and Windows certification roadmap.

Candidates who already hold the IBM Certified Database Administrator – DB2 V8.1 for Linux, UNIX, and Windows certification may opt to take the **DB2 9 for Linux, UNIX, and Windows Database Administration Upgrade** exam (Exam 736) to acquire the IBM Certified Database Administrator – DB2 9 for Linux, UNIX, and Windows certification. This exam, which is half the length and half the cost of the **DB2 9 for Linux, UNIX, and Windows Database Administration** exam (Exam 731), is designed to test a candidate's knowledge of the new features and functions that are available in DB2 9. Essentially, the upgrade exam provides certified DB2 Version 8.1 DBAs an accelerated approach for acquiring an equivalent Version 9 certification. This accelerated approach is outlined in Figure 1–2.

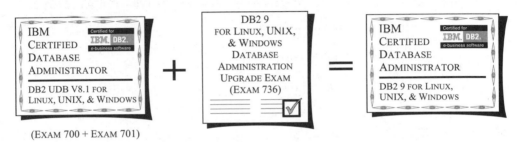

Figure 1–2: The accelerated approach for acquiring IBM Certified Database Administrator – DB2 9 for Linux, UNIX, and Windows certification.

DB2 9 for Linux, UNIX, and Windows Database Administration Upgrade exam (Exam 736) Objectives

The **DB2 9 for Linux, UNIX, and Windows Database Administration Upgrade** exam (Exam 736) consists of 38 multiple-choice questions, and candidates have 60 minutes to complete the exam. A score of 55% or higher is required to pass.

The primary objectives that the **DB2 9 for Linux, UNIX, and Windows Database Administration Upgrade** exam (Exam 736) is designed to cover are as follows (the percentages after each section title reflect the approximate distribution of the total question set across the sections):

Section 1 - Server Management (29%)

- Understand the functionality of the AUTOCONFIGURE command

- Ability to manually configure communications (emphasis on IPv6)

- Ability to enable automatic maintenance

- Ability to enable the Self-Tuning Memory Manager

- Ability to enable Utility Throttling

Section 2 - Data Placement (21%)

- Knowledge of the new default behavior of the CREATE DATABASE command

- Ability to create and manage Automatic Storage table spaces

- Knowledge of Table Partitioning

- Knowledge of Data Row Compression

Section 3 - XML Concepts (13%)

- Ability to use XML data types

- Ability to create and manage XML indexes

- Ability to use basic XML functions (for example, XMLPARSE, XMLSERIALIZE, XMLVALIDATE, and XMLQUERY)

- Knowledge of basic XQuery fundamentals

- Ability to use DB2 utilities with XML data

Section 4 - Analyzing DB2 Activity (16%)

- Ability to use DB2's troubleshooting utilities (db2bfd, db2mtrk, and db2pd)

- Ability to monitor deadlocks

- Ability to use Administrative Routines and SNAPSHOT functions

Section 5 - High Availability (10.5%)

- Ability to use the RECOVER DATABASE command

- Knowledge of High Availability Disaster Recovery (HADR)

Section 6 - Security (10.5%)

- Knowledge of DB2 9's new authentication types

- Understanding of Label Based Access Control (LBAC)

Taking the DB2 9 for Linux, UNIX, and Windows Database Administration Upgrade exam (Exam 736)

When you are confident that you are ready to take the **DB2 9 for Linux, UNIX, and Windows Database Administration Upgrade** exam (Exam 736), your next step is to contact an IBM-authorized testing vendor. The DB2 9 certification exams are administered by Pearson VUE, by Thompson Prometric, and, in rare, cases by IBM (for example, IBM administers the DB2 9 certifications free of charge at some of the larger database conferences, such as the International DB2 User's Group North American conference). However, before you contact either testing vendor, you should visit their Web site (*www.vue.com/ibm* and *www.2test.com*, respectively) and use the navigation tools provided there to locate a testing center that is convenient for you. Once you have located a testing center, you can then contact the vendor and make arrangements to take the certification exam. (Contact information for the testing vendors can also be found on their respective Web sites; in some cases, you can schedule an exam online.)

You must make arrangements to take a certification exam at least 24 hours in advance, and when you contact the testing vendor, you should be ready to provide the following information:

- Your name (as you want it to appear on your certification certificate).

- An identification number (if you have taken an IBM certification exam before, this is the number assigned to you at that time; if not, the testing vendor will supply one)

- A telephone number where you can be reached

- A fax number

- The mailing address to which you want all certification correspondence, including your certification welcome package, to be sent

- Your billing address, if it is different from your mailing address

- Your email address

- The number that identifies the exam you wish to take (for example, Exam 736)

- The method of payment (credit card or check) you wish to use, along with any relevant payment information (such as credit card number and expiration date)

- Your company's name (if applicable)

- The testing center where you would like to take the certification exam

- The date when you would like to take the certification exam

Before you make arrangements to take a certification exam, you should have paper and pencil or pen handy so that you can write down the test applicant identification number the testing center will assign you. You will need this information when you arrive at the testing center to take the certification exam. (If time permits, you will be sent a letter of confirmation containing the number of the certification exam you have been scheduled to take, along with corresponding date, time, and location information; if you register within 48 hours of the scheduled testing date, you will not receive a letter.)

If you have already taken one or more of the certification exams offered, you should make the testing vendor aware of this and ask them to assign you the same applicant identification number that was used before. This will allow the certification team at IBM to quickly recognize when you have met all the exam requirements for a particular certification role. (If you were assigned a unique applicant identification number each time you took an exam, you should go to the IBM Professional Certification Member Web site (*www.ibm.com/certify/members*) and select Member Services to combine all of your exam results under one ID.)

The DB2 9 for Linux, UNIX, and Windows Database Administration Upgrade exam (Exam 736) costs $75 (in the United States). Scheduling procedures vary according to how you choose to pay for the exam. If you decide to pay by credit card, you can make arrangements to take the exam immediately after providing the testing vendor with the appropriate information. However, if you elect to pay by check, you will be required to wait until the check has been received and payment has been confirmed before you will be allowed to make arrangements to take the exam. (Thompson Prometric recommends that if you pay by check, you write your registration ID on the front and contact them seven business days after the check is mailed. At that time, they should have received and confirmed your payment, and you should be able to make arrangements to take the exam for which you have paid.) If, for some reason, you need to reschedule or cancel your testing appointment after it is made, you must do so at least 24 hours before your scheduled test time. Otherwise, you will still be charged the price of the exam.

On the day you are scheduled to take a certification exam, you should arrive at the testing center at least 15 minutes before the scheduled start time, to sign in. As part of the sign-in process, you will be asked to provide the applicant identification number you were assigned when you made arrangements to take the exam and two forms of identification. One form of identification must feature a recent photograph, and the other must show your signature. Examples of valid forms of identification include a driver's license (photograph) and a credit card (signature).

Once you are signed in, the exam administrator will instruct you to enter the testing area and select an available workstation. The exam administrator will then enter your name and identification number into the workstation you have chosen, provide you with a pencil and some paper, and instruct you to begin the exam when you are ready.

As soon as you complete the exam and submit it for grading, the IBM Certification Exam testing software will evaluate your answers and produce a score report that indicates whether you passed the exam. Each certification exam is broken into sections, and regardless of whether you pass or fail, you should take a few moments to review the score you received for each section. This information can help you evaluate your strengths and weaknesses; if you failed to pass the exam, it can help you identify the areas you should spend some time reviewing before you take the exam again.

Shortly after you take a certification exam (usually within five working days), the testing vendor sends your results, along with your demographic data (e.g., name, address, phone number) to the IBM Certification Group for processing. If you passed the exam, you will receive credit toward the certification role the exam was designed for, and if the exam you took completes the requirements that have been outlined for a particular certification role, you will receive an email (at the email address you provided during registration) containing a copy of the IBM Certification Agreement and a welcome package that includes a certificate suitable for framing (in the form of a PDF file), camera-ready artwork of the IBM certification logo, and guidelines for using the "IBM Certified" mark. (If this email cannot be delivered, the welcome package will be sent to you via regular mail.) You can also receive a printed certificate, along with a wallet-sized certificate, via regular mail by going to the Web site referenced in the email you receive and requesting it—you will be asked to provide your Fulfillment ID and Validation Number (also provided in the email) as verification that you have met the requirements for certification.

Upon receipt of the welcome package, you are officially certified, and can begin using the IBM Professional Certification title and trademark. (You should receive the IBM Certification Agreement and welcome package within four to six weeks after IBM processes the exam results.) However, if you failed to pass the exam and you still wish to become certified, you must make arrangements to take it again (including paying the testing fee again). There are no restrictions on the number of times you can take a particular certification exam; however, you cannot take the same certification exam more than two times within a 30-day period.

Server Management

Twenty nine percent (29%) of the DB2 9 for Linux, UNIX, and Windows Database Administration Upgrade exam (Exam 736) is designed to test your knowledge about basic DB2 server management. The questions that make up this portion of the exam are intended to evaluate the following:

- Your understanding of the AUTOCONFIGURE command

- Your ability to manually configure client/server connectivity

- Your ability to use Automatic Maintenance

- Your ability to throttle utilities

- Your ability to use DB2's Self-Tuning Memory Manager (STMM)

This chapter is designed to introduce you to the various concepts you need to be familiar with in order to manage a DB2 9 server. This chapter will also provide you with information about some of the tools that are available for server management.

Instance and Database Configurations

DB2 sees the world as a hierarchy of objects. Workstations (or servers) on which DB2 has been installed occupy the highest level of this hierarchy. When any edition of DB2 is installed on a workstation, program files for a background process known as the DB2 Database Manager are physically copied to a specific location on that workstation, and in most cases, an instance of the DB2 Database Manager is created. Instances occupy the second level in the hierarchy and are responsible for managing system resources and databases that fall under their control. Databases make up the third level in the hierarchy and are responsible for managing the storage, modification, and retrieval of data.

During normal operation, the behavior of the DB2 Database Manager is controlled, in part, by a collection of values that define the DB2 operating environment. Some of these values are operating system environment variables, and others are special DB2-specific system-level values known as environment or registry variables. Along with this comprehensive set of registry variables DB2 uses an extensive array of configuration parameters to control how system resources are allocated and utilized on behalf of an instance and a database. Unfortunately, the default values provided for many of these configuration parameters were produced with very simple systems in mind. (The goal was for DB2 to run out of the box, on virtually any platform, not for DB2 to run optimally on the platform on which it is installed.) Thus, even though the default values provided for these configuration parameters are sufficient to meet most database needs, you can usually greatly improve overall system and application performance simply by changing the values of one or more configuration parameters.

Whenever an instance is created, a corresponding DB2 Database Manager configuration file is also created and initialized as part of the instance creation process. Each DB2 Database Manager configuration file is made up of approximately 85 different parameter values, and most control the amount of system resources that are allocated to a single DB2 Database Manager instance. Likewise, each time a new database is created a corresponding database configuration file is created and initialized. Each database configuration file is made up of approximately 105 different parameters, and just as most DB2 Database Manager instance configuration parameters control the amount of system resources that will be allocated to a single DB2 Database Manager instance, many of the database configuration file parameters control the amount of system resources that will be allocated to a database during normal operation.

The Configuration Advisor

With such a broad range of configuration parameters to choose from, deciding where to start and what changes to make can be difficult. Fortunately, DB2 comes packaged with a tool to help you get started; that tool is the Configuration Advisor.

The Configuration Advisor is designed to capture specific information about your database environment and recommend or make changes to configuration parameters based on the information provided.

You can activate the Configuration Advisor by selecting the Configuration Advisor action from the Databases menu found in the Control Center. Figure 2–1 shows how the Configuration Advisor looks when it is first activated.

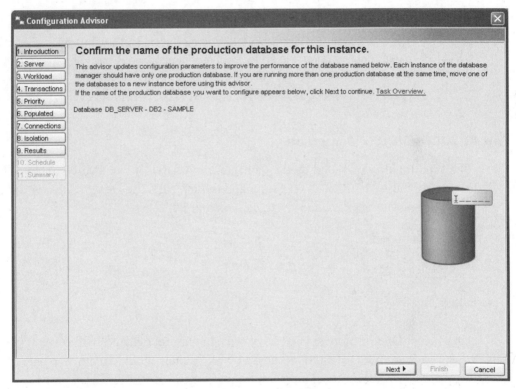

Figure 2–1: The Configuration Advisor dialog.

Once the Configuration Advisor wizard is activated, you simply follow the directions shown on each panel presented to describe your server environment and to explain what a typical transaction workload for your database looks like. When you have provided the information requested, the Configuration Advisor will recommend changes that should improve overall performance if made to instance and/or database configuration parameters. At that time, the "Finish" push button displayed in the lower right corner of the wizard (see Figure 2–1) will be enabled, and when this button is selected, the recommended configuration parameter changes may be applied.

In DB2 9, the Configuration Advisor is automatically invoked whenever you create a database using the Create Database Wizard. (This behavior can be changed by assigning the value NO to the DB2_ENABLE_AUTOCONFIG_DEFAULT registry variable.)

The Configuration Advisor (and the AUTOCONFIGURE command) makes configuration and buffer pool recommendations based on the assumption that only one database is defined per instance.

The AUTOCONFIGURE Command

The functionality provided by the Configuration Advisor can also be obtained by executing the AUTOCONFIGURE command (which calls the Design Advisor under the covers). The basic syntax for this command is:

```
AUTOCONFIGURE
USING [[Keyword] [Value] ,...]
APPLY [DB ONLY | DB AND DBM | NONE]
```

where:

Keyword   One or more special keywords that are recognized by the AUTOCONFIGURE command. Valid values include mem_percent, workload_type, num_stmts, tpm, admin_priority, is_populated, num_local_apps, num_remote_apps, isolation, and bp_resizable.

Value   Identifies the value associated with the keyword provided. Table 2.1 lists the values that are valid for each keyword recognized by the AUTOCONFIGURE command.

Table 2.1 AUTOCONFIGURE Command Keywords and Values		
Keyword	**Valid Values / Default**	**Description**
mem_percent	1–100 Default: 25	Percentage of available server memory (RAM) the DB2 Database Manager is to use when performing database operations.
workload_type	simple, complex, mixed Default: mixed	The type of workload that is usually run against the database. Valid values are as follows: simple—database is used primarily to resolve queries (for example, data warehousing); complex—database is used primarily for transaction processing (for example, order entry and OLTP); and mixed—database is used to resolve queries and to process transactions. Simple workloads tend to be I/O-intensive and mostly transactions, whereas complex workloads tend to be CPU-intensive and mostly queries.
num_stmts	1–1,000,000 Default: 10	Average number of SQL statements executed within a single transaction (i.e., between commits). NOTE: If unknown, choose a number greater than 10.
tpm	1–200,000 Default: 60	Average number of transactions executed per minute (estimated). NOTE: The DB2 Performance Monitor can help you get a more accurate TPM measurement.
admin_priority	performance, recovery, both Default: both	Type of activity for which the database should be optimized. Valid values include the following: performance—database should be optimized for transaction performance (slower backup/recovery); recovery—database should be optimized for backup and recovery (slower transaction performance); or both—database should be optimized for both transaction performance and backup/recovery (both are equally important).
is_populated	yes, no Default: yes	Indicates whether the database currently contains data. Valid values are as follows: yes—the database contains data; and no—the database does not contain data.
num_local_apps	0–5,000 Default: 0	Number of local applications that will be connected to the database at one time.

Table 2.1 AUTOCONFIGURE Command Keywords and Values (continued)		
Keyword	**Valid Values / Default**	**Description**
num_remote_apps	0–5,000 Default: 10	Number of remote applications that will be connected to the database at one time. Allocating memory to handle all connections needed (both local and remote) ensures that users never have to wait for an existing connection to be terminated before they can get connected. However, over-allocating memory for connections can result in wasted resources. The DB2 Performance Monitor can help you determine how many connections are actually acquired within a specified time frame.
isolation	RR, RS, CS, UR Default: RR	Isolation level used by most applications that access the database. Valid values include the following: RR—Repeatable Read (large number of locks acquired for long periods of time); RS—Read Stability (small number of locks acquired for long periods of time); CS—Cursor Stability (large number of locks acquired for short periods of time); and UR—Uncommitted Read (no locks acquired).
bp_resizeable	yes, no Default: yes	Are buffer pools resizable?

If the APPLY DB ONLY clause is specified with the AUTOCONFIGURE command, database configuration and buffer pool changes recommended by the Design Advisor will be applied to the appropriate database configuration file; if the APPLY DB AND DBM clause is specified, database configuration and buffer pool changes recommended will be applied to the database configuration file, and instance configuration changes recommended will be applied to the appropriate DB2 Database Manager configuration file. If the APPLY NONE clause is specified instead, change recommendations will be displayed, but not applied.

Thus, if you wanted to determine the best configuration to use for an OLTP database named SAMPLE that uses resizable buffer pools and is populated, and you wanted to review any configuration changes recommended before applying them to the appropriate database configuration file, you could do so by executing an AUTOCONFIGURE command that looks like this:

```
AUTOCONFIGURE USING workload_type complex,
  is_populated yes,
  bp_resizable yes
APPLY NONE
```

On the other hand, if you wanted to determine the best configuration to use if 60 percent of a system's memory will be available for the DB2 Database Manager to use when performing database operations, the instance controlls only one database (named SAMPLE), and you wanted to automatically update the appropriate configuration files to reflect any configuration changes recommended, you could do so by executing an AUTOCONFIGURE command that looks like this:

```
AUTOCONFIGURE USING mem_percent 60 APPLY DB AND DBM
```

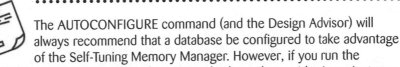

The AUTOCONFIGURE command (and the Design Advisor) will always recommend that a database be configured to take advantage of the Self-Tuning Memory Manager. However, if you run the AUTOCONFIGURE command against a database that resides in an instance where the SHEAPTHRES configuration parameter has been assigned a value other than zero, the sort memory heap database configuration parameter (SORTHEAP) will not be configured for automatic tuning. Therefore, you must execute the command UPDATE DATABASE MANAGER CONFIGURATION USING SHEAPTHRES 0 before you execute the AUTOCONFIGURE command if you want to enable sort memory tuning.

Configuring Communications

In a typical client/server environment, databases stored on a server are accessed by applications stored on remote client workstations using what is known as a distributed connection. In addition to providing client applications with a way to access a centralized database located on a remote server, a distributed connection also provides a way for administrators to manage databases and servers remotely.

When DB2 is installed on a workstation, it is automatically configured to take advantage of any communications protocols that have been set up for that particular workstation (provided the protocols found are recognized by DB2). At that time, information about each supported communications protocol available is collected and stored in the configuration files for both the DAS instance and the default instance as they are created. However, this information is not updated automatically when a new protocol is activated or when an existing protocol is reconfigured. Instead, you must manually configure communications for each instance before such changes will be reflected.

Manually Configuring Communications

The easiest way to manually configure communications or make communications configuration changes is by using the Setup communications dialog, which can be activated by selecting the appropriate action from the Instances menu found in the Control Center. Figure 2–2 shows how the Setup communications dialog might be used to configure the TCP/IP protocol for a particular instance.

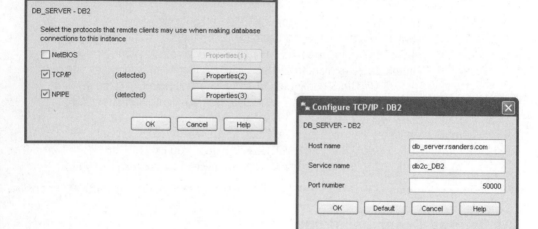

Figure 2–2: The Setup communications dialog and the Configure TCP/IP dialog.

If you choose to manually configure communications without using the Setup communications dialog, the steps you must follow can vary according to the communications protocol being used. For example, if you wanted to configure a server to use TCP/IP, you would have to perform the following steps (in any order):

1. Assign the value TCPIP to the DB2COMM registry variable.

    Whenever you manually configure communications for a server, you must update the value of the DB2COMM registry variable before an instance can begin using the desired communications protocol. The value assigned to the DB2COMM registry variable is used to determine which communications managers will be activated when the DB2 Database Manager for a particular instance is started.

The DB2COMM registry variable is assigned the value TCPIP by executing a db2set command that looks something like this:

```
db2set DB2COMM=TCPIP
```

2. Assign the name of the TCP/IP port that the database server will use to receive communications from remote clients to the *svcename* parameter of the DB2 Database Manager configuration file.

   The *svcename* parameter should be set to the service name associated with the main connection port so that when the database server is started, it can determine which port to listen on for incoming connection requests. This parameter is set by executing an UPDATE DATABASE MANAGER CONFIGURATION command that looks something like this:

   ```
   UPDATE DBM CFG USING SVCENAME db2c_db2inst1
   ```

3. Update the services file on the database server, if appropriate.

   The TCP/IP services file identifies the ports that server applications will listen on for client requests. If you specified a service name in the *svcename* parameter of the DB2 Database Manager configuration file, the appropriate service name-to-port number/protocol mapping must be added to the services file on the server. (If you specified a port number in the *svcename* parameter, the services file does not need to be updated.)

   The default location of the services file depends on the operating system being used: on UNIX-based systems, the services file is located in: /etc/services; on Windows servers, the services file is located in %SystemRoot%\system32\drivers\etc. An entry in the services file for a DB2 database server might look something like this:

   ```
   db2c_db2inst1        50001/tcp
   ```

Cataloging and Uncataloging a Node

Nodes (servers) are usually cataloged implicitly whenever a remote database is cataloged via the Configuration Assistant. However, if you want to explicitly catalog a node (i.e., add an entry to the node directory for a particular server), you can do so by executing a CATALOG...NODE command that corresponds to the communications protocol that will be used to access the server being cataloged. Several forms of the CATALOG...NODE command are available, including the following:

- CATALOG LOCAL NODE

- CATALOG LDAP NODE

- CATALOG NAMED PIPE NODE

- CATALOG TCPIP NODE

The syntax for all of these commands is very similar, the major difference being that many of the options available with each are specific to the communications protocol for which the command has been tailored. Because TCP/IP is probably the most common communications protocol in use today, let's take a look at the syntax for that form of the CATALOG...NODE command.

The syntax for the CATALOG TCPIP NODE command is:

```
CATALOG <ADMIN> [TCPIP | TCPIP4 | TCPIP6] NODE [NodeName]
REMOTE [IPAddress | HostName]
SERVER [ServiceName | PortNumber]
<SECURITY SOCKS>
<REMOTE INSTANCE [InstanceName]>
<SYSTEM [SystemName]>
<OSTYPE [SystemType]>
<WITH "[Description]">
```

where:

NodeName   Identifies the alias to be assigned to the node to be cataloged. This is an arbitrary name created on the user's workstation and is used to identify the node.

IPAddress   Identifies the IP address of the server where the remote database you are trying to communicate with resides.

HostName   Identifies the host name, as it is known to the TCP/IP network. (This is the name of the server where the remote database you are trying to communicate with resides.)

ServiceName   Identifies the name of the service with which the DB2 Database Manager instance on the server uses to communicate.

PortNumber   Identifies the port number with which the DB2 Database Manager instance on the server uses to communicate.

InstanceName   Identifies the name of the server instance to which an attachment is to be made.

SystemName   Identifies the DB2 system name that is used to identify the server workstation.

SystemType   Identifies the type of operating system being used on the server workstation. The following values are valid for this parameter: AIX, WIN, HPUX, SUN, OS390, OS400, VM, VSE, and LINUX.

Description   A comment used to describe the node entry that will be made in the node directory for the node being cataloged. The description must be enclosed by double quotation marks.

Thus, if you wanted to catalog a node for an AIX server named DB2HOST that has a DB2 instance named DB2INST1 that listens on port 60000 and assign it the alias RMT_SERVER, you could do so by executing a CATALOG TCPIP NODE command that looks something like this:

```
CATALOG TCPIP NODE rmt_server
REMOTE db2host
SERVER 60000
OSTYPE AIX
WITH "A remote AIX TCP/IP node"
```

On the other hand, if you wanted to catalog a node for a Linux server that has the IPv6 address 1080:0:0:0:8:800:200C:417A and a DB2 instance named DB2INST1 that is listening on port 60000 and assign it the alias IPV6_SERVER, you could do so by executing a CATALOG TCPIP NODE command that looks something like this:

```
CATALOG TCPIP NODE ipv6_server
REMOTE 1080:0:0:0:8:800:200C:417A
SERVER 60000
OSTYPE LINUX
WITH "A remote Linux TCP/IP node"
```

Automatic Maintenance

Although the Task Center can be used to schedule routine maintenance operations, in some cases it can be time-consuming to determine whether and when to run some of the more resource-intensive maintenance utilities available. With automatic maintenance (a new feature introduced in DB2 9), you specify your maintenance objectives, and the DB2 Database Manager will use the objectives you have identified to determine whether one or more maintenance activities need to be performed. If it is determined that a maintenance operation is required, that operation will be carried out during the next available maintenance window (a maintenance window is a time period, specified by you, in which all automatic maintenance activities are to be performed).

Automatic maintenance can be used to perform the following maintenance operations:

- **Create a backup image of the database.** Automatic database backup provides users with a solution to help ensure their database is being backed up both properly and regularly, without their having to worry about when to back up or having any knowledge of the syntax for the BACKUP command.

- **Data defragmentation (table or index reorganization).** This maintenance activity can increase the efficiency with which the DB2 Database Manager accesses tables. Automatic reorganization manages offline table and index reorganization without users having to worry about when and how to reorganize their data.

- **Data access optimization (running RUNSTATS).** The DB2 Database Manager updates the system catalog statistics on the data in a table, the data in a table's indexes, or the data in both a table and its indexes. The DB2 Optimizer uses these statistics to determine which path to use to access data in response to a query. Automatic statistics collection attempts to improve the performance of the database by maintaining up-to-date table statistics. The goal is to allow the DB2 Optimizer to always choose an access plan based on accurate statistics.

- **Statistics profiling.** Automatic statistics profiling advises when and how to collect table statistics by detecting outdated, missing, and incorrectly specified statistics and by generating statistical profiles based on query feedback.

When a DB2 9 database is created, automatic maintenance is enabled by default; enablement of individual automatic maintenance features is controlled using various automatic maintenance-specific database configuration parameters. Table 2.2 lists the automatic maintenance-specific database configuration parameters available.

Table 2.2 DB2 Automatic Maintenance-Specific Database Configuration Parameters		
Parameter	Value Range / Default	Description
auto_maint	ON, OFF Default: ON	Enables or disables automatic maintenance for the database. This is the parent of all the other automatic maintenance database configuration parameters (*auto_db_backup*, *auto_tbl_maint*, *auto_runstats*, *auto_stats_prof*, *auto_prof_upd*, and *auto_reorg*). When this parameter is disabled, all of its children parameters are also disabled, but their settings, as recorded in the database configuration file, do not change. When this parent parameter is enabled, recorded values for its children parameters take effect.
auto_db_backup	ON, OFF Default: ON	Enables or disables automatic backup operations for the database.
auto_tbl_maint	ON, OFF Default: ON	Enables or disables automatic table maintenance operations for the database. This parameter is the parent of all table maintenance parameters (*auto_runstats*, *auto_stats_prof*, *auto_prof_upd*, and *auto_reorg*). When this parameter is disabled, all of its children parameters are also disabled, but their settings, as recorded in the database configuration file, do not change. When this parent parameter is enabled, recorded values for its children parameters take effect.
auto_runstats	ON, OFF Default: ON	Enables or disables automatic table RUNSTATS operations for the database.
auto_stats_prof	ON, OFF Default: ON	Enables or disables automatic statistical profile generation for the database.
auto_prof_upd	ON, OFF Default: ON	Enables or disables automatic runstats profile updating for the database.
auto_reorg	ON, OFF Default: ON	Enables or disables automatic table and index reorganization for the database.
Adapted from Table 64 and Table 65 on pages 269–273 of the DB2 9 Performance Guide manual		

The *auto_maint* database configuration parameter enables or disables automatic maintenance for a database so it must be assigned the value ON before any automatic maintenance operation can be performed; the *auto_tbl_maint* database configuration parameter enables or disables automatic table maintenance for a database so it must be assigned the value ON before automatic table maintenance operations can be performed.

Utility Throttling

Automatic maintenance activities (backup, statistics collection, statistics profiling, and table/index reorganization) consume resources and may affect the performance of your database when they are run. Additionally, offline database backup and table/index reorganization operations can restrict access to tables, indexes, or the entire database. To minimize system impact, the resource usage of some automatic maintenance activities can be regulated with DB2's adaptive utility throttling system.

The adaptive utility throttling system allows maintenance utilities to be run concurrently during critical periods, while keeping their performance impact on production workloads within acceptable limits. The following maintenance operations can be throttled:

- Statistics collection

- Backup operations

- Rebalancing operations

- Asynchronous index cleanups

The value assigned to the *util_impact_lim* DB2 Database Manager configuration parameter limits the amount of performance degradation throttled utilities can have on a production workload. To define the impact policy for *all* throttled utilities, you simply assign the *util_impact_lim* configuration parameter any value between 1 and 100. For example, to configure an instance so that an automatic backup operation invocation will not impact the system workload by more than 10 percent, you would assign the *util_impact_lim* configuration parameter the value 10 by executing an UPDATE DATABASE MANAGER command that looks like this:

```
UPDATE DATABASE MANAGER USING UTIL_IMPACT_LIM 10
```

As you would expect, a throttled utility will usually take longer to complete than an unthrottled utility. If you find that a utility is running for an excessively long time, you can increase the value assigned to the *util_impact_lim* configuration parameter, or you can disable throttling altogether by setting the *util_impact_lim* configuration parameter to 100. (If *util_impact_lim* is set to 100, utility invocations are not throttled. In this case, the utilities can complete faster, but they most likely will have an undesirable impact on workload performance.)

Although the impact policy for throttled utilities is defined by the value assigned to the *util_impact_lim* configuration parameter, this policy can be overridden by using a special option that is available with the commands that are used are to invoke throttled utilities. The syntax for this special option is:

```
UTIL_IMPACT_PRIORITY <Priority>
```

where:

Priority   Specifies the amount of throttling to which the utility is to be subjected. A value of 100 represents the highest priority; a value of 1 represents the lowest. If no *Priority* is specified, the utility will be executed with a default priority of 50. (All utilities at the same priority undergo the same amount of throttling, and utilities at lower priorities are throttled more than those at higher priorities.)

For example, if you wanted to backup a database named SALES and have the backup operation run throttled with a priority of 20, you could do so by executing a BACKUP DATABASE command that looks something like this:

```
BACKUP DB sales UTIL_IMPACT_PRIORITY 20
```

If the command used to invoke a throttled utility is executed without the UTIL_IMPACT_PRIORITY option, the utility will run unthrottled, even if the *util_impact_lim* configuration parameter has been assigned a value other than 100.

Obtaining Information About Running Utilities

If you want to find out which, if any, utilities are running against an instance and what their throttling impact priority is, you can do so by executing the LIST UTILITIES command. The syntax for this command is:

```
LIST UTILITIES
<SHOW DETAIL>
```

So if you started an unthrottled backup operation for a database named SAMPLE, you could obtain detailed information about this operation by executing a LIST UTILITIES command that looks like this:

```
LIST UTILITIES SHOW DETAIL
```

And when this command is executed, the information produced would look something like this:

```
ID                                = 1
Type                              = BACKUP
Database Name                     = SAMPLE
Partition Number                  = 0
Description                       = offline db
Start Time                        = 06/02/2007 10:35:31.442019
State                             = Executing
Invocation Type                   = User
Throttling:
    Priority                      = Unthrottled
Progress Monitoring:
    Estimated Percentage Complete = 46
        Total Work                = 49310404 bytes
        Completed Work            = 22696620 bytes
        Start Time                = 06/02/2007 10:35:31.466054
```

Changing a Running Utility's Impact Priority

If you want to change the impact priority (level of throttling) of a utility that is already running, you can do so by executing the SET UTIL_IMPACT_PRIORITY command. With this command, you can

- throttle a running utility that was started in unthrottled mode,

- unthrottle a running throttled utility (disable throttling), and

- reprioritize a running throttled utility (this is useful if multiple simultaneous throttled utilities are running and one is more important than the others).

The syntax for the SET UTIL_IMPACT_PRIORITY command is:

```
SET UTIL_IMPACT_PRIORITY [UtilityID]
TO [Priority]
```

where:

UtilityID   Identifies the running utility, by ID, whose priority is to be changed. (The ID assigned to a running utility can be obtained by executing the LIST UTILITIES command.)

Priority   Specifies an instance-level limit on the impact associated with running the utility specified. A value of 100 represents the highest priority; a value of 1 represents the lowest. Setting *Priority* to 0 will force a throttled utility to continue running unthrottled; setting *Priority* to a non-zero value will force an unthrottled utility to continue running in throttled mode.

Thus, if you wanted to force the unthrottled backup operation that information was obtained for earlier (with the LIST UTILITIES command) to continue running in throttled mode, you could do so by executing a SET UTIL_IMPACT_PRIORITY command that looks like this:

```
SET UTIL_IMPACT_PRIORITY 1 TO 20
```

When this statement is executed, the backup operation should have no more than a 20 percent average impact on the total workload being processed by the server.

Self-Tuning Memory Manager

Although utility throttling can help reduce the impact the execution of a utility has on production workloads, how well (or poorly) workloads perform often depends on how resources such as memory are utilized by the server. And as we saw earlier, the DB2 Database Manager configuration and database configuration parameters control how system resources are allocated for instances and databases. In DB2 9, a new memory tuning feature, known as the Self-Tuning Memory Manager (STMM), simplifies the task of configuring memory-related database parameters by automatically setting values for these parameters after measuring and analyzing how well each DB2 memory consumer is using the allocated memory available. The following memory consumers can be enabled for self-tuning:

- Buffer pools (controlled by the ALTER BUFFERPOOL and CREATE BUFFERPOOL statements)

- Package cache (controlled by the *pckcachesz* configuration parameter)

- Locking memory (controlled by the *locklist* and *maxlocks* configuration parameters)

- Sort memory (controlled by the *sheapthres_shr* and the *sortheap* configuration parameters)

- Database shared memory (controlled by the *database_memory* configuration parameter)

When a database is not enabled for self-tuning, the entire database will use a specified amount of memory, distributing it across the database memory consumers as required. However, when a database has been enabled for self-tuning, the memory tuner responds to significant changes in database workload characteristics, adjusting the values of memory configuration parameters and buffer pool sizes to optimize performance. If the current workload requirements are high, and there is sufficient free memory on the system, more memory will be consumed by the database. Once the workload's memory requirements drop, or if the amount of free memory available on the system becomes too low, some database shared memory is released.

Self-tuning is enabled for a database by assigning the value ON to the *self_tuning_mem* database configuration parameter. This is done by executing the UPDATE DATABASE CONFIGURATION command. (The database has to be stopped and restarted before the change will take effect.)

Specific memory areas that are controlled by a memory configuration parameter can be enabled for self-tuning by assigning the value AUTOMATIC to the parameter, using the UPDATE DATABASE CONFIGURATION command; you can enable buffer pools for self-tuning by setting their size to AUTOMATIC, using either the CREATE BUFFERPOOL or the ALTER BUFFERPOOL SQL statement. However, because the memory tuner trades memory resources between different memory consumers, there must be at least two memory consumers enabled for self-tuning in order for self-tuning to be active. (Not to mention the fact that the database itself must have the *self_tuning_mem* database configuration parameter set to ON.)

In order for automatic tuning of sort memory to occur, the sheapthres_shr database configuration must be assigned the value AUTOMATIC and the sheapthres DB2 Database Manager configuration parameter must be set to 0.

Once a database and two or more memory consumers have been configured for self-tuning, the current memory configuration for the database can be obtained by executing the GET DATABASE CONFIGURATION command. Changes made by self-tuning are recorded in memory tuning log files, which reside in the *stmmlog* subdirectory of the instance. (The first file created will be assigned the name *stmm.0.log*, the second will be assigned the name *stmm.1.log*, and so on.) Each memory tuning log file contains summaries of the resource demands for each memory consumer at the time a tuning operation was performed. Tuning intervals can be determined by examining the timestamps for the entries made in the memory tuning log files.

Practice Questions

Question 1

Which of the following is NOT a valid keyword for the AUTOCONFIGURE command?

○ A. mem_percent

○ B. workload_type

○ C. num_apps

○ D. isolation

Question 2

Which statement regarding the AUTOCONFIGURE command is NOT valid?

○ A. The DB2_ENABLE_AUTOCONFIG_DEFAULT registry variable must be set to ON in order for the AUTOCONFIGURE command to be run successfully.

○ B. If the APPLY DB ONLY clause is specified with the AUTOCONFIGURE command, database configuration and buffer pool changes recommended by the Design Advisor will be applied to the appropriate database configuration file.

○ C. The AUTOCONFIGURE command will only make recommendations based on the assumption of a single database per instance.

○ D. If the APPLY NONE clause is specified with the AUTOCONFIGURE command, change recommendations will be displayed, but not applied.

Question 3

Which of the following commands will successfully catalog a node for a Linux server that has the IP address 1800:0:0:0:6:400:200C:217A and a DB2 instance named DB2INST1 that is listening on port 60000 and assign it the alias RMT_SERVER?

○ A. CATALOG TCPIP NODE rmt_server
     REMOTE 1800:0:0:0:6:400:200C:217A
     SERVER 6000
     OSTYPE LINUX

○ B. CATALOG TCPIP2 NODE rmt_server
     REMOTE 1800:0:0:0:6:400:200C:217A
     SERVER 6000
     OSTYPE LINUX

○ C. CATALOG TCPIP4 NODE rmt_server
     REMOTE 1800:0:0:0:6:400:200C:217A
     SERVER 6000
     OSTYPE LINUX

○ D. CATALOG TCPIP6 NODE rmt_server
     REMOTE 1800:0:0:0:6:400:200C:217A
     SERVER 6000
     OSTYPE LINUX

Question 4

A DB2 Version 8.2 database named PAYROLL was successfully migrated to DB2 9. Which of the following commands will activate automatic table and index reorganization for the database?

○ A. UPDATE DB CFG FOR payroll USING AUTO_MAINT ON AUTO_REORG
     ON;

○ B. UPDATE DB CFG FOR payroll USING AUTO_MAINT ON
     AUTO_TBL_MAINT ON;

○ C. UPDATE DB CFG FOR payroll USING AUTO_TBL_MAINT ON
     AUTO_REORG ON;

○ D. UPDATE DB CFG FOR payroll USING AUTO_MAINT ON
     AUTO_TBL_MAINT ON AUTO_REORG ON;

Question 5

A database administrator wants to collect statistics automatically for a database named SALES. Which of the following database configuration parameters does NOT have to be set to ON for automatic statistics collection to be enabled?

○ A. AUTO_MAINT

○ B. AUTO_STATS_PROF

○ C. AUTO_TBL_MAINT

○ D. AUTO_RUNSTATS

Question 6

A database administrator obtained the following information about a DB2 9 database that was created recently by executing the command GET DB CFG FOR personnel (Note: output has been reduced to conserve space.):

```
Automatic maintenance          (AUTO_MAINT) = OFF
Automatic database backup      (AUTO_DB_BACKUP) = OFF
Automatic table maintenance    (AUTO_TBL_MAINT) = OFF
Automatic runstats             (AUTO_RUNSTATS) = OFF
Automatic statistics profiling (AUTO_STATS_PROF) = OFF
Automatic profile updates      (AUTO_PROF_UPD) = OFF
Automatic reorganization       (AUTO_REORG) = OFF
```

Which of the following commands will enable automatic statistics profiling for the PERSONNEL database?

○ A. UPDATE DB CFG FOR personnel USING AUTO_MAINT ON
       AUTO_STATS_PROF ON

○ B. RESET DB CFG FOR personnel;
       UPDATE DB CFG FOR personnel USING AUTO_MAINT ON;

○ C. UPDATE DB CFG FOR personnel USING AUTO_MAINT ON
       AUTO_TBL_MAINT ON

○ D. RESET DB CFG FOR personnel;
       UPDATE DB CFG FOR personnel USING AUTO_STATS_PROF ON;

Question 7

A database administrator wants to ensure that when statistics are collected for a table named EMPLOYEE, the operation will not impact a production workload by more than 10 percent. Which two of the following commands must be executed in order to achieve this objective?

❑ A. UPDATE DBM CFG USING UTIL_IMPACT_LIM 10

❑ B. UPDATE DBM CFG USING UTIL_IMPACT_LIM ON

❑ C. UPDATE DBM CFG USING UTIL_IMPACT_LIM 100

❑ D. RUNSTATS ON TABLE employee UTIL_IMPACT_PRIORITY 10

❑ E. RUNSTATS ON TABLE employee UTIL_IMPACT_PRIORITY 90

Question 8

A LIST UTILITIES SHOW DETAIL command returned the following output:

```
ID                              = 1
Type                            = BACKUP
Database Name                   = SAMPLE
Partition Number                = 0
Description                     = offline db
Start Time                      = 06/02/2007 10:35:31.442019
State                           = Executing
Invocation Type                 = User
Throttling:
    Priority                    = 20
Progress Monitoring:
    Estimated Percentage Complete = 46
        Total Work              = 49310404 bytes
        Completed Work          = 22696620 bytes
        Start Time              = 06/02/2007 10:35:31.466054
```

Which of the following commands will allow the backup operation to continue running unthrottled?

○ A. SET UTIL_IMPACT_PRIORITY 1 TO 0

○ B. SET UTIL_IMPACT_LIM 1 TO 0

○ C. SET UTIL_IMPACT_PRIORITY 1 TO 100

○ D. SET UTIL_IMPACT_LIM 1 TO 100

Question 9

If the following commands are executed in the order shown:

```
UPDATE DBM CFG USING UTIL_IMPACT_LIM 75;
BACKUP DATABASE sales UTIL_IMPACT_PRIORITY;
```

By what percentage will the backup operation impact production workloads while it executes?

○ A. 25%

○ B. 50%

○ C. 75%

○ D. 100%

Question 10

Which of the following memory consumers can NOT be tuned automatically by the Self-Tuning Memory Manager as the database workload changes?

○ A. Buffer pools

○ B. Locking memory

○ C. Utility memory

○ D. Database shared memory

Question 11

Where are changes made by the Self-Tuning Memory Manager recorded?

○ A. In memory tuning log files.

○ B. In the DB2 Diagnostics Log File

○ C. In the Administration Notification Log

○ D. In the Journal

Question 12

Which of the following operations does NOT have to be performed before the Self-Tuning Memory Manager will be configured to manage all possible memory tuning conditions?

○ A. Set the database configuration parameter SELF_TUNING_MEM to ON

○ B. Set all buffer pool sizes to AUTOMATIC

○ C. Set the registry variable DB2_SELF_TUNING_MEM to ON

○ D. Set the PCKCACHESZ, LOCKLIST, MAXLOCKS, SHEAPTHRES_SHR, SORTHEAP, and DATABASE_MEMORY configuration parameters to AUTOMATIC

Question 13

A DB2 Version 8.2 database named ACCOUNTING was successfully migrated to DB2 9. Which of the following commands will activate the Self-Tuning Memory Manager for the database and identify which memory consumers have been configured for self-tuning?

○ A. db2set SELF_TUNING_MEM=ON;

ACTIVATE DATABASE accounting;

db2set -all;

○ B. UPDATE DB CFG FOR accounting USING SELF_TUNING_MEM ON;

ACTIVATE DATABASE accounting;

GET DB CFG FOR accounting SHOW DETAIL;

○ C. ACTIVATE DATABASE accounting;

GET DB CFG FOR accounting SHOW DETAIL;

○ D. UPDATE DB CFG FOR accounting USING SELF_TUNING_MEM ON;

ACTIVATE DATABASE accounting;

LIST MEMORY SETTINGS FOR accounting;

Question 14

A database administrator wants to use the Self-Tuning Memory Manager to manage memory requirements of a database named ORDERS. Which two of the following commands must be executed before the Self-Tuning Memory Manager can be used to automatically set a soft limit on the total amount of database shared memory that can be used by sort memory consumers at any one time?

❏ A. UPDATE DBM CFG USING SHEAPTHRES 0

❏ B. UPDATE DBM CFG USING SHEAPTHRES AUTOMATIC

❏ C. UPDATE DB CFG FOR orders USING SHEAPTHRES AUTOMATIC

❏ D. UPDATE DB CFG FOR orders USING SHEAPTHRES_SHR 0

❏ E. UPDATE DB CFG FOR orders USING SHEAPTHRES_SHR AUTOMATIC

Answers

Question 1

The correct answer is **C**. The keywords that are recognized by the AUTOCONFIGURE command are: mem_percent, workload_type, num_stmts, tpm, admin_priority, is_populated, num_local_apps, num_remote_apps, isolation, and bp_resizable.

Question 2

The correct answer is **A**. In DB2 9, the Configuration Advisor is automatically invoked whenever you create a database using the Create Database Wizard. This behavior can be changed by assigning the value NO to the DB2_ENABLE_AUTOCONFIG_DEFAULT registry variable. (The value assigned to the DB2_ENABLE_AUTOCONFIG_DEFAULT registry variable has no affect on the AUTOCONFIGURE command.)

Question 3

The correct answer is **D**. Nodes (servers) are usually cataloged implicitly whenever a remote database is cataloged via the Configuration Assistant. However, if you want to explicitly catalog (i.e., add an entry to the node directory for a particular server), you can do so by executing a CATALOG...NODE command that corresponds to the communications protocol that will be used to access the server being cataloged. The syntax for the CATALOG TCPIP NODE command is:

```
CATALOG <ADMIN> [TCPIP | TCPIP4 | TCPIP6] NODE [NodeName]
REMOTE [IPAddress | HostName]
SERVER [ServiceName | PortNumber]
<SECURITY SOCKS>
<REMOTE INSTANCE [InstanceName]>
<SYSTEM [SystemName]>
<OSTYPE [SystemType]>
<WITH "[Description]">
```

where:

NodeName   Identifies the alias to be assigned to the node to be cataloged. This is an arbitrary name created on the user's workstation and is used to identify the node.

IPAddress   Identifies the IP address of the server where the remote database you are trying to communicate with resides.

HostName	Identifies the host name, as it is known to the TCP/IP network. (This is the name of the server where the remote database you are trying to communicate with resides.)
ServiceName	Identifies the name of the service with which the DB2 Database Manager instance on the server uses to communicate.
PortNumber	Identifies the port number with which the DB2 Database Manager instance on the server uses to communicate.
InstanceName	Identifies the name of the server instance to which an attachment is to be made.
SystemName	Identifies the DB2 system name that is used to identify the server workstation.
SystemType	Identifies the type of operating system being used on the server workstation. The following values are valid for this parameter: AIX, WIN, HPUX, SUN, OS390, OS400, VM, VSE, and LINUX.
Description	A comment used to describe the node entry that will be made in the node directory for the node being cataloged. The description must be enclosed by double quotation marks.

Thus, if you wanted to catalog a node for a Linux server that has the IPv6 address 1800:0:0:0:6:400:200C:217A and a DB2 instance named DB2INST1 that is listening on port 60000 and assign it the alias RMT_SERVER, you could do so by executing a CATALOG TCPIP NODE command that looks something like this:

```
CATALOG TCPIP NODE rmt_server
REMOTE 1800:0:0:0:6:400:200C:217A
SERVER 60000
OSTYPE LINUX
```

Question 4

The correct answer is **D**. The *auto_maint* database configuration parameter enables or disables automatic maintenance for a database; this is the parent of all other automatic maintenance database configuration parameters (*auto_db_backup*, *auto_tbl_maint*, *auto_runstats*, *auto_stats_prof*, *auto_prof_upd*, and *auto_reorg*). When this parameter is assigned the value OFF, all of its children parameters are disabled, but their settings, as recorded in the database configuration file, do not change. When this parameter is assigned the value ON, recorded values for its children parameters take effect.

The *auto_tbl_maint* database configuration parameter enables or disables automatic table maintenance for a database; this is the parent of all table maintenance parameters (*auto_runstats*, *auto_stats_prof*, *auto_prof_upd*, and *auto_reorg*). When this parameter is set to OFF, all of its children parameters are disabled, but their settings, as recorded in the database configuration file, do not change. When this parameter is assigned the value ON, recorded values for its children parameters take effect.

The *auto_reorg* database configuration parameter enables or disables automatic table and index reorganization for a database. When this parameter is assigned the value ON, table and index reorganization operations are performed automatically, when necessary.

Question 5

The correct answer is **B**. The *auto_maint* database configuration parameter enables or disables automatic maintenance for a database so it must be assigned the value ON before any automatic maintenance operation can be performed; the *auto_tbl_maint* database configuration parameter enables or disables automatic table maintenance for a database so it must be assigned the value ON before automatic table maintenance operations can be performed; the *auto_runstats* database configuration parameter enables or disables automatic table RUNSTATS operations for a database so it must be assigned the value ON before automatic statistics collection for a database will be performed.

The *auto_stats_prof* database configuration parameter enables or disables automatic statistical profile generation for a database so it does not have to be assigned the value ON before automatic statistics collection for a database will be performed.

Question 6

The correct answer is **D**. When a DB2 9 database is created, automatic maintenance is enabled by default; when the database configuration parameters are reset to their system defaults (by executing the RESET DATABASE CONFIGURATION command), the AUTO_MAINT, AUTO_DB_BACKUP, and AUTO_TBL_MAINT configuration parameters are assigned the value ON. The *auto_stats_prof* database configuration parameter enables or disables automatic statistical profile generation for a database. When this parameter is assigned the value ON, statistical profile generation operations are performed automatically, when necessary.

Question 7

The correct answers are **A** and **D**. The value assigned to the UTIL_IMPACT_LIM DB2 Database Manager configuration parameter limits the amount of performance degradation throttled utilities can have on a production workload. To define the impact policy for *all* throttled utilities, you simply assign the UTIL_IMPACT_LIM configuration parameter any value between 1 and 100; If UTIL_IMPACT_LIM is set to 100, utilities are not throttled.

Although the impact policy for throttled utilities is defined by the value assigned to the UTIL_IMPACT_LIM configuration parameter, this policy can be overridden by using a special option that is available with the commands that are used are to invoke throttled utilities. The syntax for this special option is:

```
UTIL_IMPACT_PRIORITY <Priority>
```

where:

Priority   Specifies the amount of throttling to which the utility is to be subjected. A value of 100 represents the highest priority; a value of 1 represents the lowest. If no *Priority* is specified, the utility will be executed with a default priority of 50. (All utilities at the same priority undergo the same amount of throttling, and utilities at lower priorities are throttled more than those at higher priorities.)

Thus, if you wanted to collect statistics for a table named EMPLOYEE and have the operation run throttled with a priority of 10, you could do so by executing a RUNSTATS command that looks something like this:

```
RUNSTATS ON TABLE employee UTIL_IMPACT_PRIORITY 10
```

Question 8

The correct answer is **A**. If you want to change the impact priority (level of throttling) of a utility that is already running, you can do so by executing the SET UTIL_IMPACT_PRIORITY command. The syntax for this command is:

```
SET UTIL_IMPACT_PRIORITY [UtilityID]
TO [Priority]
```

where:

UtilityID   Identifies the running utility, by ID, whose priority is to be changed. (The ID assigned to a running utility can be obtained by executing the LIST UTILITIES command.)

Priority   Specifies an instance-level limit on the impact associated with running the utility specified. A value of 100 represents the highest priority; a value of 1 represents the lowest. Setting *Priority* to 0 will force a throttled utility to continue running unthrottled; setting *Priority* to a non-zero value will force an unthrottled utility to continue running in throttled mode.

Thus, if you wanted force a throttled backup operation that has been assigned a utility ID of 1 to continue running unthrottled, you could do so by executing a SET UTIL_IMPACT_PRIORITY command that looks like this:

```
SET UTIL_IMPACT_PRIORITY 1 TO 0
```

Question 9

The correct answer is **B**. Because the UTIL_IMPACT_PRIORITY option was used when the BACKUP DATABASE command was executed, but no priority value was specified, the backup operation was assigned a default priority of 50, which means that the backup operation will impact other production workloads by 50 percent.

Question 10

The correct answer is **C**. When a database has been enabled for self tuning, the memory tuner responds to significant changes in database workload characteristics, adjusting the values of memory configuration parameters and buffer pool sizes to optimize performance. The following memory consumers can be enabled for self tuning:

- Buffer pools (controlled by the ALTER BUFFERPOOL and CREATE BUFFERPOOL statements)

- Package cache (controlled by the *pckcachesz* configuration parameter)

- Locking memory (controlled by the *locklist* and *maxlocks* configuration parameters)

- Sort memory (controlled by the *sheapthres_shr* and the *sortheap* configuration parameter)

- Database shared memory (controlled by the *database_memory* configuration parameter)

Question 11

The correct answer is **A**. Changes made by the Self Tuning Memory Manager are recorded in memory tuning log files, which reside in the *stmmlog* subdirectory of the instance. (The first file created will be assigned the name *stmm.0.log*, the second will be assigned the name *stmm.1.log*, and so on.) Each memory tuning log file contains summaries of the resource demands for each memory consumer at the time a tuning operation was performed. Tuning intervals can be determined by examining the timestamps for the entries made in the memory tuning log files.

Question 12

The correct answer is **C**. Self-tuning is enabled for a database by assigning the value ON to the *self_tuning_mem* database configuration parameter. Specific memory areas that are controlled by a memory configuration parameter can be enabled for self-tuning by assigning the value AUTOMATIC to the parameter, using the UPDATE DATABASE CONFIGURATION command; you can enable buffer pools for self-tuning by setting their size to AUTOMATIC, using either the CREATE BUFFERPOOL or the ALTER BUFFERPOOL SQL statement. The following memory consumers can be enabled for self tuning:

- Buffer pools

- Package cache (controlled by the *pckcachesz* configuration parameter)

- Locking memory (controlled by the *locklist* and *maxlocks* configuration parameters)

- Sort memory (controlled by the *sheapthres_shr* and the *sortheap* configuration parameter)

- Database shared memory (controlled by the *database_memory* configuration parameter)

Question 13

The correct answer is **B**. Self-tuning is enabled for a database by assigning the value
ON to the *self_tuning_mem* database configuration parameter. This is done by executing
the UPDATE DATABASE CONFIGURATION command. (The database has to be stopped
and restarted before the change will take effect.) Once a database has been configured
for self-tuning, the current memory configuration for the database can be obtained by
executing the GET DATABASE CONFIGURATION command.

Question 14

The correct answers are **A** and **E**. In order for automatic tuning of sort memory to occur,
the *sheapthres_shr* database configuration must be assigned the value AUTOMATIC *and*
the *sheapthres* DB2 Database Manager configuration parameter must be set to 0.

CHAPTER 3

Data Placement

Twenty one percent (21%) of the DB2 9 for Linux, UNIX, and Windows Database Administration Upgrade exam (Exam 736) is designed to test your ability to create a DB2 9 database, as well as to test your knowledge of the methods used to create and manage table spaces and range-partitioned tables. The questions that make up this portion of the exam are intended to evaluate the following:

- Your knowledge of the new default behavior of the CREATE DATABASE command

- Your knowledge of the characteristics of SMS, DMS, and Automatic Storage table spaces

- Your ability to create and manage Automatic Storage table spaces

- Your ability to create range-partitioned tables

- Your knowledge of data row compression

This chapter is designed to walk you through the DB2 9 database creation process, and to provide you with an overview of the various types of table spaces that can be constructed once a database exists. This chapter is also designed to show you how to construct range-partitioned tables, as well as use data row compression to reduce storage space requirements for a table.

Creating a DB2 9 Database

There are two ways to create a DB2 9 database: by executing the CREATE DATABASE command by using the Create Database Wizard – which is essentially a graphical user interface (GUI) for the CREATE DATABASE command. In its simplest form, the syntax for the CREATE DATABASE command is:

```
CREATE [DATABASE | DB] [DatabaseName]
```

where:

DatabaseName   Identifies a unique name that is to be assigned to the database once it is created.

The only value you must provide when executing this command is a name to assign to the new database. This name

- can consist of only the characters **a** through **z**, **A** through **Z**, **0** through **9**, **@**, **#**, **$**, and _ (underscore);

- cannot begin with a number;

- cannot begin with the letter sequences "SYS," "DBM," or "IBM"; and

- cannot be the same as the name already assigned to another database within the same instance.

Of course, a much more complex form of the CREATE DATABASE command that provides you with much more control over database parameters is available, and we will examine it shortly. But for now, let's look at what happens when this form of the CREATE DATABASE command is executed.

What Happens When a DB2 9 Database Is Created

Regardless of how the process is initiated, whenever a new DB2 9 database is created, the following tasks are performed, in the order shown:

1. All directories and subdirectories needed are created in the appropriate location.

Information about every DB2 9 database created is stored in a special hierarchical directory tree. Where this directory tree is actually created is determined by information provided with the CREATE DATABASE command—if no location information is provided, this directory tree is created in the location specified by the *dftdbpath* DB2 Database Manager configuration parameter associated with the instance under which the database is being created. The root directory of this hierarchical tree is assigned the name of the instance with which the database is associated. This directory will contain a subdirectory that has been assigned a name corresponding to the partition's node. If the database is a partitioned database, this directory will be named NODExxxx, where xxxx is the unique node number that has been assigned to the partition; if the database is a nonpartitioned database, this directory will be named NODE0000. The node-name directory, in turn, will contain one subdirectory for each database that has been created, along with one subdirectory that includes the containers that are used to hold the database's data.

The name assigned to the subdirectory that holds the containers used to house the database's data is the same as that specified for the database; the name assigned to the subdirectory that contains the base files for the database corresponds to the database token that is assigned to the database during the creation process (the subdirectory for the first database created will be named SQL00001, the subdirectory for the second database will be named SQL00002, and so on). Figure 3–1 illustrates how this directory hierarchy typically looks in a nonpartitioned database environment.

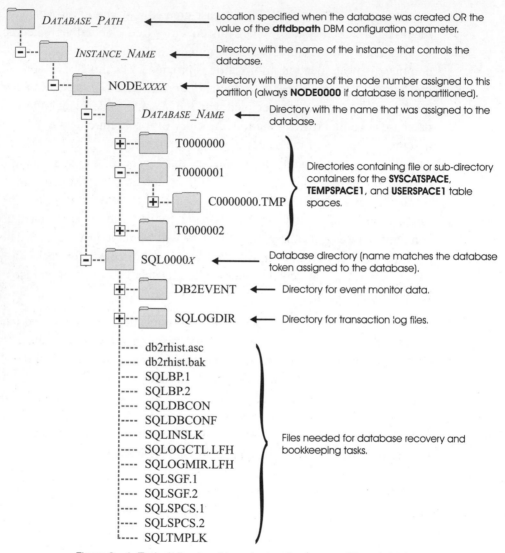

Figure 3—1: Typical directory hierarchy tree for a nonpartitioned database.

Never attempt to modify this directory structure or any of the files stored in it. Such actions could destroy one or more databases or make them unusable.

2. Files needed for management, monitoring, and database recovery are created.

   After the subdirectory that was assigned the name of the database's token is created, the following files are created in it:

   db2rhist.asc This file contains historical information about backup operations, restore operations, table load operations, table reorganization operations, table space alterations, and similar database changes (i.e., the recovery history file).

   db2rhist.bak This file is a backup copy of db2rhist.asc.

   SQLBP.1 This file contains buffer pool information.

   SQLBP.2 This file is a backup copy of SQLBP.1.

   SQLDBCON This file contains database configuration information.

   SQLDBCONF This file is a backup copy of SQLDBCON.

   SQLINSLK This file contains information that is used to ensure that the database is assigned to only one instance of the DB2 Database Manager.

   SQLOGCTL.LFH This file contains information about active transaction log files. Recovery operations use information stored in this file to determine how far back in the logs to begin the recovery process.

   SQLOGMIR.LFH This file is a mirrored copy of SQLOGCTL.LFH.

   SQLSGF.1 This file contains storage path information associated with automatic storage.

   SQLSGF.2 This file is a backup copy of SQLSGF.1.

   SQLSPCS.1 This file contains table space information.

   SQLSPCS.2 This file is a backup copy of SQLSPCS.1.

   SQLTMPLK This file contains information about temporary table spaces.

   Two subdirectories named DB2EVENT and SQLOGDIR are also created; a detailed deadlocks event monitor is created and stored in the DB2EVENT subdirectory, and three files named S0000000.LOG, S0000001.LOG, and

S0000002.LOG are created and stored in the SQLLOGDIR subdirectory. These three files are used to store transaction log records as SQL operations are performed against the database.

3. A buffer pool is created for the database.

    During the database creation process, a buffer pool is created and assigned the name IBMDEFAULTBP. By default, on Linux and UNIX platforms, this buffer pool is 1,000 4K (kilobyte) pages in size; on Windows platforms, this buffer pool is 250 4K pages in size. The actual memory used by this buffer pool (and for that matter, by any other buffer pools that may exist) is allocated when the first connection to the database is established and freed when all connections to the database have been terminated.

4. Two regular table spaces and one system temporary table space are created.

    Immediately after the buffer pool IBMDEFAULTBP is created, three table spaces are created and associated with this buffer pool. These three table spaces are as follows:

    *   A regular table space named SYSCATSPACE, which is used to store the system catalog tables and views associated with the database

    *   A regular table space named USERSPACE1, which is used to store all user-defined objects (such as tables, indexes, and so on) along with user data, index data, and long value data

    *   A system temporary table space named TEMPSPACE1, which is used as a temporary storage area for operations such as sorting data, reorganizing tables, and creating indexes

    Unless otherwise specified, SYSCATSPACE and USERSPACE1 will be DMS FILE table spaces, and TEMPSPACE1 will be an SMS table space; characteristics for each of these table spaces can be provided as input to the CREATE DATABASE command or the Create Database Wizard.

5. The system catalog tables and views are created.

    After the table space SYSCATSPACE is created, a special set of tables, known as the system catalog tables, are constructed within that table space. The DB2 Database Manager uses the system catalog tables to keep track of such information as database object definitions, database object dependencies, database object privileges, column data types, table constraints, and object relationships. A set of system catalog views is created along with the system catalog tables, and these views are typically used when accessing data stored in the system catalog tables. The system catalog tables and views cannot be modified with SQL statements (however, their contents can be viewed). Instead, they are modified by the DB2 Database Manager whenever one of the following events occurs:

    *   A database object (such as a table, view, or index) is created, altered, or dropped.

    *   Authorizations or privileges are granted or revoked.

    *   Statistical information is collected for a table.

    *   Packages are bound to the database.

    In most cases, the complete characteristics of a database object are stored in one or more system catalog tables when the object is created. However, in some cases, such as when triggers and constraints are defined, the actual SQL used to create the object is stored instead.

6. The database is cataloged in the system and local database directory (a system or local database directory is created first if it does not already exist.)

    DB2 uses a set of special files to keep track of where databases are stored and to provide access to those databases. Because the information stored in these files is used like the information stored in an office-building directory is used, they are referred to as directory files. Whenever a database is created, these directories are updated with the database's name and alias. If specified, a comment and code set values are also stored in these directories.

7. The database configuration file for the database is initialized.

   Some of the parameters in the database configuration file (such as code set, territory, and collating sequence) will be set using values that were specified as input for the CREATE DATABASE command or the Create Database Wizard; others are assigned system default values.

8. Four schemas are created.

   Once the system catalog tables and views are created, the following schemas are created: SYSIBM, SYSCAT, SYSSTAT, and SYSFUN. A special user named SYSIBM is made the owner of each.

9. A set of utility programs is bound to the database.

   Before some of the DB2 9 utilities available can work with a database, the packages needed to run those utilities must be created. Such packages are created by binding a set of predefined DB2 Database Manager bind files to the database (the bind files used are stored in the utilities bind list file *db2ubind.lst*).

10. Authorities and privileges are granted to the appropriate users.

    To connect to and work with a particular database, a user must have the authorities and privileges needed to use that database. Therefore, whenever a new database is created, unless otherwise specified, the following authorities and privileges are granted:

    - Database Administrator (DBADM) authority as well as CONNECT, CREATETAB, BINDADD, CREATE_NOT_FENCED, IMPLICIT_SCHEMA, and LOAD privileges are granted to the user who created the database.

    - USE privilege on the table space USERSPACE1 is granted to the group PUBLIC.

    - CONNECT, CREATETAB, BINDADD, and IMPLICIT_SCHEMA privileges are granted to the group PUBLIC.

- SELECT privilege on each system catalog table is granted to the group PUBLIC.

- EXECUTE privilege on all procedures found in the SYSIBM schema is granted to the group PUBLIC.

- EXECUTE WITH GRANT privilege on all functions found in the SYSFUN schema is granted to the group PUBLIC.

- BIND and EXECUTE privileges for each successfully bound utility are granted to the group PUBLIC.

11. Several autonomic features are enabled.

    To help make management easy, whenever a new database is created, the following features are enabled:

    - Automatic Maintenance (database backups, table and index reorganization, data access optimization, and statistics profiling)

    - Self-Tuning Memory Manager (package cache, locking memory, sort memory, database shared memory, and buffer pool memory)

    - Utility throttling

    - The Health Monitor

12. The Configuration Advisor is launched.

    The Configuration Advisor is a tool designed to help you tune performance and balance memory requirements for a database by suggesting which configuration parameters to modify based on information you provide about the database. In DB2 9, the Configuration Advisor is automatically invoked whenever you create a database, unless the default behavior is changed by assigning the value NO to the DB2_ENABLE_AUTOCONFIG_DEFAULT registry variable.

The Complete CREATE DATABASE Command

When the simplest form of the CREATE DATABASE command is executed, the characteristics of the database created, such as the storage and transaction logging method used, are determined by several predefined defaults. If you wish to change any of the default characteristics, you must specify one or more options available when executing the CREATE DATABASE command. The complete syntax for this command is:

```
CREATE [DATABASE | DB] [DatabaseName] <AT DBPARTITIONNUM>
```

or

```
CREATE [DATABASE | DB] [DatabaseName]
<AUTOMATIC STORAGE [YES | NO]>
<ON [StoragePath ,...] <DBPATH [DBPath]>>
<ALIAS [Alias]>
<USING CODESET [CodeSet] TERRITORY [Territory]>
<COLLATE USING [CollateType]>
<PAGESIZE [4096 | Pagesize <K>]>
<NUMSEGS [NumSegments]>
<DFT_EXTENT_SZ [DefaultExtSize]>
<RESTRICTIVE>
<CATALOG TABLESPACE [TS_Definition]>
<USER TABLESPACE [TS_Definition]>
<TEMPORARY TABLESPACE [TS_Definition]>
<WITH "[Description]">
<AUTOCONFIGURE <USING [Keyword] [Value] ,...>
    <APPLY [DB ONLY | DB AND DBM | NONE>>
```

where:

DatabaseName   Identifies the unique name that is to be assigned to the database to be created.

StoragePath   If AUTOMATIC STORAGE YES is specified (the default), identifies one or more storage paths that are to be used to hold table space containers used by automatic storage. Otherwise, identifies the location (drive or directory) where the directory hierarchy and files associated with the database to be created are to be physically stored.

DBPath   If AUTOMATIC STORAGE YES is specified (the default), identifies the location (drive or directory) where the directory hierarchy and metadata files associated with the database to be created are to be physically stored. (If this parameter is not specified, and automatic storage is used, the metadata files will be stored in the first storage path specified in the *StoragePath* parameter.)

Alias   Identifies the alias to be assigned to the database to be created.

CodeSet Identifies the code set to be used for storing data in the database to be created. (In a DB2 9 database, each single-byte character is represented internally as a unique number between 0 and 255. This number is referred to as the code point of the character; the assignments of code points to every character in a particular character set are called the code page; and the International Organization for Standardization term for a code page is code set.)

Territory Identifies the territory to be used for storing data in the database to be created.

CollateType Specifies the collating sequence (i.e., the sequence in which characters are ordered for the purpose of sorting, merging, and making comparisons) that is to be used by the database to be created. The following values are valid for this parameter: COMPATABILITY, IDENTITY, IDENTITY_16BIT, UCA400_NO, UCA400_LSK, UCA400_LTH, NLSCHAR, and SYSTEM.

NumSegments Specifies the number of directories that are to be created and used to store files for the default SMS table space used by the database to be created (TEMPSPACE1).

DefaultExtSize Specifies the default extent size to be used whenever a table space is created and no extent size is specified during the creation process.

Description A comment used to describe the database entry that will be made in the database directory for the database to be created. The description must be enclosed by double quotation marks.

Keyword One or more keywords recognized by the AUTOCONFIGURE command. Valid values include mem_percent, workload_type, num_stmts, tpm, admin_priority, is_populated, num_local_apps, num_remote_apps, isolation, and bp_resizable. Refer to the *DB2 9 Command Reference* for more information on how the AUTOCONFIGURE command is used.

Value   Identifies the value that is to be associated with the *Keyword* specified.

TS_Definition Specifies the definition that is to be used to create the table space that will be used to hold the system catalog tables (SYSCATSPACE), user-defined objects (USERSPACE1), and/or temporary objects (TEMPSPACE1).

The syntax used to define a system managed (SMS) table space is:

```
MANAGED BY SYSTEM
USING ('[Container]' ,...)
<EXTENTSIZE [ExtentSize]>
<PREFETCHSIZE [PrefetchSize]>
<OVERHEAD [Overhead]>
<TRANSFERRATE [TransferRate]>
```

The syntax used to define a database managed (DMS) table space is:

```
MANAGED BY DATABASE
USING ([FILE | DEVICE] '[Container]' NumberOfPages ,...)
<EXTENTSIZE [ExtentSize]>
<PREFETCHSIZE [PrefetchSize]>
<OVERHEAD [Overhead]>
<TRANSFERRATE [TransferRate]>
<AUTORESIZE [NO | YES]>
<INCREASESIZE [Increment] <PERCENT | K | M | G>>
<MAXSIZE [NONE | MaxSize <K | M | G>]>
```

And the syntax used to define an automatic storage table space is:

```
MANAGED BY AUTOMATIC STORAGE
<EXTENTSIZE [ExtentSize]>
<PREFETCHSIZE [PrefetchSize]>
<OVERHEAD [Overhead]>
<TRANSFERRATE [TransferRate]>
<AUTORESIZE [NO | YES]>
<INITIALSIZE [InitialSize] <K | M | G>>
<INCREASESIZE [Increment] <PERCENT | K | M | G>>
<MAXSIZE [NONE | MaxSize <K | M | G>]>
```

where:

Container   Identifies one or more containers to be used to store data that will be assigned to the table space specified. For SMS table spaces, each container specified must identify a valid directory; for DMS FILE containers, each container specified must identify a valid file; and for DMS DEVICE containers, each container specified must identify an existing device.

NumberOfPages   Specifies the number of pages to be used by the table space container.

ExtentSize   Specifies the number of pages of data that will be written in a round-robin fashion to each table space container used.

PrefetchSize   Specifies the number of pages of data that will be read from the specified table space when data prefetching is performed.

Overhead   Identifies the input/output (I/O) controller overhead and disk-seek latency time (in number of milliseconds) associated with the containers that belong to the specified table space.

TransferRate   Identifies the time, in number of milliseconds, that it takes to read one page of data from a table space container and store it in memory.

InitialSize   Specifies the initial size an autoresizing DMS or an automatic storage table space should be.

Increment   Specifies the amount by which a table space that has been enabled for automatic resizing will be increased when the table space becomes full and a request for space is made.

MaxSize   Specifies the maximum size to which a table space that has been enabled for automatic resizing can be increased to.

If the RESTRICTIVE clause is specified, the RESTRICT_ACCESS database configuration parameter for the database being created will be set to YES, and no privileges will be granted to the group PUBLIC.

Suppose you wanted to create a DB2 database that has the following characteristics:

- Will be physically located on drive E:.

- Will not use automatic storage.

- Will be assigned the name SAMPLEDB.

- Will recognize the United States/Canada code set. (The code page, along with the territory, is used to convert alphanumeric data to binary data that is stored in the database.)

- Will use a collating sequence that is based on the territory used (which in this case is United States/Canada).

- Will not automatically be accessible to the group PUBLIC.

- Will store the system catalog in a DMS table space that uses the file SYSCATSPACE.DAT as its container. (This file is stored on drive E: and is capable of holding up to 5,000 pages that are 4K in size.)

In this case, you would execute a CREATE DATABASE command that looks something like this:

```
CREATE DATABASE sampledb
AUTOMATIC STORAGE NO
ON E:
USING CODESET 1252 TERRITORY US
COLLATE USING SYSTEM
PAGESIZE 4096
RESTRICTIVE
CATALOG TABLESPACE MANAGED BY DATABASE
   (FILE 'E:\syscatspace.dat', 5000)
```

Table Spaces

Table spaces are used to control where data is physically stored and to provide a layer of indirection between database objects (such as tables, indexes, and views) and one or more containers (i.e., directories, files, or raw devices) in which the object's data actually resides. A single table space can span many containers, but each container can belong to only one table space. When a table space spans multiple containers, data is written in a round-robin fashion (in groups of pages called extents) to each container assigned to that table space; this helps balance data across all containers that belong to a given table space.

Two types of table spaces can exist: system managed space (SMS) table spaces and database managed space (DMS) table spaces. With SMS table spaces, only directory containers can be used for storage and the operating system's file manager is responsible for controlling how that space is used. The SMS storage model consists of many files (each representing a table, index, or long data object) that reside within the file system space—the user decides on the location of the files, the DB2 Database Manager assigns the files their names, and the file system is responsible for managing their growth. With DMS table spaces, only file and/or device containers can be used for storage, and the DB2 Database Manager is responsible for controlling how the space is used.

If a database is enabled for automatic storage, one other type of table space—an automatic storage table space—can exist. Although at first glance, automatic storage table spaces appear to be a third type of table space, they are really just an extension of SMS and DMS table spaces: regular and large table spaces are created as DMS table spaces with one or more file containers; system and user temporary table spaces are created as SMS table spaces with one or more directory containers. Unlike when SMS and DMS table spaces are defined, no container definitions are needed for automatic storage table spaces; the DB2 Database Manager assigns containers to automatic storage table spaces automatically.

Creating New Table Spaces

Earlier, we saw that when a DB2 database is created, one buffer pool named IBMDEFAULTBP is created, and three table spaces are created and associated with this buffer pool as part of the database initialization process. Additional table spaces can be created by executing the CREATE TABLESPACE SQL statement. The basic syntax for this statement is:

```
CREATE
<REGULAR | LARGE | SYSTEM TEMPORARY | USER TEMPORARY>
TABLESPACE [TablespaceName]
<PAGESIZE [PageSize] <K>>
MANAGED BY SYSTEM USING ('[Container]' ,...)
<EXTENTSIZE [ExtentPages | ExtentSize <K | M | G>]>
<PREFETCHSIZE [AUTOMATIC | PrefetchPages |
     PrefetchSize <K | M | G>]>
<BUFFERPOOL [BufferPoolName]>
<<NO> FILE SYSTEM CACHING>
<DROPPED TABLE RECOVERY <ON | OFF>>
```

or

```
CREATE
<REGULAR | LARGE | SYSTEM TEMPORARY | USER TEMPORARY>
TABLESPACE [TablespaceName]
<PAGESIZE [PageSize] <K>>
MANAGED BY DATABASE USING ([FILE | DEVICE] '[Container]'
     [ContainerPages | ContainerSize <K | M | G>] ,...)
<AUTORESIZE [YES | NO]>
<INCREASESIZE [IncSize <PERCENT | K | M | G>]>
<MAXSIZE [NONE | MaxSize <K | M | G>]>
<EXTENTSIZE [ExtentPages | ExtentSize <K | M | G>]> <PREFETCHSIZE
[AUTOMATIC | PrefetchPages |
     PrefetchSize <K | M | G>]>
<BUFFERPOOL [BufferPoolName]>
<<NO> FILE SYSTEM CACHING>
<DROPPED TABLE RECOVERY <ON | OFF>>
```

or

```
CREATE
<REGULAR | LARGE | SYSTEM TEMPORARY | USER TEMPORARY>
TABLESPACE [TablespaceName]
<PAGESIZE [PageSize] <K>>
MANAGED BY AUTOMATIC STORAGE
<AUTORESIZE [YES | NO]>
<INITIALSIZE [InitSize <K | M | G>]>
<INCREASESIZE [IncSize <PERCENT | K | M | G>]>
<MAXSIZE [NONE | MaxSize <K | M | G>]>
<EXTENTSIZE [ExtentPages | ExtentSize <K | M | G>]> <PREFETCHSIZE
[AUTOMATIC | PrefetchPages |
     PrefetchSize <K | M | G>]>
<BUFFERPOOL [BufferPoolName]>
<<NO> FILE SYSTEM CACHING>
<DROPPED TABLE RECOVERY <ON | OFF>>
```

where:

TablespaceName   Identifies the name that is to be assigned to the table space to be created.

PageSize   Specifies the size that each page used by the table space being created is to be. The following values are valid for this parameter: 4,096; 8,192; 16,384 or 32,768 bytes—if the suffix K (for kilobytes) is provided, this parameter must be set to 4, 8, 16, or 32. Unless otherwise specified, pages used by table spaces are 4K in size.

Container   Identifies, by name, one or more containers that are to be used to store the data associated with the table space to be created.

ContainerPages   Identifies the amount of storage, by number of pages, that is to be preallocated for the container(s) identified in the *Container* parameter.

ContainerSize   Identifies the amount of storage that is to be preallocated for the container(s) identified in the *Container* parameter. The value specified for this parameter is treated as the total number of bytes, unless the letter K (for kilobytes), M (for megabytes), or G (for gigabytes) is also specified. (If a *ContainerSize* value is specified, it is converted to a *ContainerPages* value using the *PageSize* value provided.)

InitSize   Identifies the amount of storage that is to be preallocated for an autoresizing DMS or an automatic storage table space.

IncSize   Identifies the amount by which a table space enabled for automatic resizing will automatically be increased when the table space is full and a request for more space is made.

MaxSize   Identifies the maximum size to which a table space enabled for automatic resizing can automatically be increased.

ExtentPages   Identifies the number of pages of data that are to be written to a single table space container before another container will be used.

ExtentSize   Identifies the amount of data that is to be written to a single table space container before another container will be used. The value specified for this parameter is treated as the total number of bytes, unless the letter K (for kilobytes), M (for megabytes), or G (for gigabytes) is also specified. (If an *ExtentSize* value is specified, it is converted to an *ExtentPages* value using the *PageSize* value provided.)

PrefetchPages   Identifies the number of pages of data that are to be read from the table space when data prefetching is performed (prefetching allows data needed by a query to be read before it is referenced so that the query spends less time waiting for I/O).

PrefetchSize   Identifies the amount of data that is to be read from the table space when data prefetching is performed. The value specified for this parameter is treated as the total number of bytes, unless the letter K (for kilobytes), M (for megabytes), or G (for gigabytes) is also specified. (If a *PrefetchSize* value is specified, it is converted to a *PrefetchPages* value using the *PageSize* value provided.)

BufferPoolName   Identifies the name of the buffer pool to be used by the table space to be created. (The page size of the buffer pool specified must match the page size of the table space to be created, or the CREATE TABLESPACE statement will fail.)

If the MANAGED BY SYSTEM version of this statement is executed, the resulting table space will be an SMS table space. On the other hand, if the MANAGED BY DATABASE version is executed, the resulting table space will be a DMS table space. Furthermore, if an SMS table space is to be created, only existing directories can be used as that table space's storage containers; if a DMS table space is to be created, only fixed-size preallocated files or physical raw devices can be used as that table space's storage containers.

Thus, if you wanted to create an SMS table space that has the name SALES_TS; consists of pages that are 4 kilobytes in size; uses the directories C:\TBSP1, C:\TBSP2, and C:\TBSP3 as its storage containers; and uses the buffer pool IBMDEFAULTBP, you could do so by executing a CREATE TABLESPACE SQL statement that looks something like this:

```
CREATE REGULAR TABLESPACE sales_ts
PAGESIZE 4096
MANAGED BY SYSTEM USING
    ('C:\tbsp1','C:\tbsp2', 'C:\tbsp3')
EXTENTSIZE 32
PREFETCHSIZE 96
BUFFERPOOL ibmdefaultbp
```

On the other hand, if you wanted to create a DMS table space that has the name PAYROLL_TS, consists of pages that are 8 kilobytes in size, uses the file DMS_TBSP.TSF, (which is 1,000 megabytes in size and resides in the directory C:\TABLESPACES) as its storage container, and uses the buffer pool PAYROLL_BP, you could do so by executing a CREATE TABLESPACE SQL statement that looks something like this:

```
CREATE REGULAR TABLESPACE payroll_ts
PAGESIZE 8K
MANAGED BY DATABASE USING
    (FILE 'C:\TABLESPACES\dms_tbsp.tsf' 1000 M)
BUFFERPOOL PAYROLL_BP
```

And finally, if you wanted to create an automatic storage table space that has the name HR_TS and uses the buffer pool IBMDEFAULTBP, you could do so by executing a CREATE TABLESPACE SQL statement that looks something like this:

```
CREATE REGULAR TABLESPACE payroll_ts
MANAGED BY AUTOMATIC STORAGE
```

If a database is enabled for automatic storage, the MANAGED BY AUTOMATIC STORAGE clause can be left out completely—its absence implies automatic storage. No container definitions are provided in this case because the DB2 Database Manager assigns containers automatically.

Modifying Existing Table Spaces

Because SMS table spaces rely on the operating system for physical storage space management, they rarely need to be modified after they have been successfully created. DMS table spaces, on the other hand, have to be monitored closely to ensure that the fixed-size preallocated file(s) or physical raw device(s) that they use for storage always have enough free space available to meet the database's needs. When the amount of free storage space available to a DMS table space becomes dangerously low (typically less than 10 percent), you can add more free space either by increasing the size of one or more of its containers or by adding one or more new containers to it. Existing table space containers can be resized, new containers can be made available to an existing table space, and an existing table space's properties can be changed by executing the ALTER TABLESPACE SQL statement. The basic syntax for this statement is:

```
ALTER TABLESPACE [TablespaceName]
[ADD | EXTEND | REDUCE | RESIZE]
    ([FILE | DEVICE] '[Container]'
    [ContainerPages | ContainerSize <K | M | G>] ,...)
```

or

```
ALTER TABLESPACE [TablespaceName]
[EXTEND | REDUCE | RESIZE]
    (ALL <CONTAINERS>
        [ContainerPages | ContainerSize <K | M | G>])
```

or

```
ALTER TABLESPACE [TablespaceName]
DROP ([FILE | DEVICE] '[Container]' ,...)
```

or

```
ALTER TABLESPACE [TablespaceName]
< PREFETCHSIZE AUTOMATIC |
    PREFETCHSIZE [PrefetchPages | PrefetchSize <K | M | G>]>
<BUFFERPOOL [BufferPoolName]>
<<NO> FILE SYSTEM CACHING>
<AUTORESIZE [NO | YES]>
<INCREASESIZE [IncSize <PERCENT | K | M | G>]>
<MAXSIZE [NONE | MaxSize <K | M | G>]>
<DROPPED TABLE RECOVERY [ON | OFF]>
<CONVERT TO LARGE>
```

where:

TablespaceName   Identifies the name assigned to the table space that is to be altered.

Container   Identifies one or more containers that are to be added to, resized, or removed from the table space specified.

ContainerPages   Identifies the amount of storage, by number of pages, that is to be added to, removed from, or allocated for all containers or the container(s) identified in the *Container* parameter.

ContainerSize   Identifies the amount of storage that is to be added to, removed from, or allocated for all containers or the container(s) identified in the *Container* parameter. The value specified for this parameter is treated as the total number of bytes, unless the letter K (for kilobytes), M (for megabytes), or G (for gigabytes) is also specified. (If a *ContainerSize* value is specified, it is converted to a *ContainerPages* value using the page size of the table space being offered.)

PrefetchPages   Identifies the number of pages of data to be read from the table space when data prefetching is performed.

PrefetchSize   Identifies the amount of data to be read from the table space when data prefetching is performed. The value specified for this parameter is treated as the total number of bytes, unless the letter K (for kilobytes), M (for megabytes), or G (for gigabytes) is also specified. (If a *PrefetchSize* value is specified, it is converted to a *PrefetchPages* value using the page size of the table space being altered.)

BufferPoolName   Identifies the name of the buffer pool to be used by the table space to be altered. (The page size of the buffer pool specified must match the page size used by the table space to be altered.)

IncSize   Identifies the amount by which a table space enabled for automatic resizing will automatically be increased when the table space is full and a request for more space is made.

MaxSize   Identifies the maximum size to which a table space enabled for automatic resizing can automatically be increased.

Thus, if you wanted a fixed-size preallocated file named NEWFILE.TSF that is 1,000 megabytes in size and resides in the directory C:\TABLESPACES, to be used as a new storage container for an existing DMS table space named PAYROLL_TS, you could do so by executing an ALTER TABLESPACE SQL statement that looks like this:

```
ALTER TABLESPACE payroll_ts
ADD (FILE 'C:\tablespaces\newfile.tsf' 1000 M)
```

On the other hand, if you wanted to modify an existing DMS table space named PAYROLL_TS so that it will grow automatically to a maximum size of 400 megabytes, you could do so by executing an ALTER TABLESPACE SQL statement that looks like this:

```
ALTER TABLESPACE payroll_ts
AUTORESIZE YES MAXSIZE 400 M
```

Range-Partitioned Tables

Although table spaces are used to control where data is physically stored and to provide a layer of indirection between database objects (such as tables, indexes, and views) and one or more containers (i.e., directories, files, or raw devices) in which the object's data actually resides, how database objects are assigned to table spaces when they are created determines how data is physically stored on disk. The physical storage of table data can be controlled even further by taking advantage of a new feature introduced in DB2 9 known as table partitioning.

Table partitioning (also referred to as range partitioning) is a data organization scheme in which table data is divided across multiple storage objects called data partitions or ranges based on values in one or more columns. Each data partition is stored separately, and the storage objects used can be in different table spaces, in the same table space, or a combination of the two. Table partitioning improves performance and eliminates the need to create a partitioned database using the Data Partitioning Feature.

Other advantages of using table partitioning include:

Easy roll-in and roll-out of data. Rolling in partitioned table data allows a new range to be easily incorporated into a partitioned table as an additional data partition. Rolling out partitioned table data allows you to easily separate ranges of data from a partitioned table for subsequent purging or archiving. Data can be quickly rolled in and out by using the ATTACH PARTITION and DETACH PARTITION clauses of the ALTER TABLE statement; once rolled in, newly attached data partitions are brought online by executing the SET INTEGRITY statement.

Easier administration of large tables. Table-level administration becomes more flexible because administrative tasks can be performed on individual data partitions. Such tasks include detaching and reattaching of a data partition, backing up and restoring individual data partitions, and reorganizing individual indexes. In addition, time-consuming maintenance operations can be shortened by breaking them down into a series of smaller operations. For example, backup operations can be performed at the data-partition level when each data partition is placed in a separate table space. Thus, it is possible to backup one data partition of a partitioned table at a time.

Flexible index placement. With table partitioning, indexes can be placed in different table spaces, allowing for more granular control of index placement.

Better query processing. In the process of resolving queries, one or more data partitions may be automatically eliminated based on the query predicates used. This functionality, known as Data Partition Elimination, improves the performance of many decision support queries because less data has to be analyzed before a result data set can be returned.

Data from a given table is partitioned into multiple storage objects based on the specifications provided in the PARTITION BY clause of the CREATE TABLE statement. The syntax for this optional clause is:

```
PARTITION BY <RANGE>
  ([ColumnName] <NULLS LAST | NULLS FIRST> ,...)
  (STARTING <FROM>
      <(> [Start | MINVALUE | MAXVALUE] < ,...)>
```

```
              <INCLUSIVE | EXCLUSIVE>
          ENDING <AT>
              <(> [End | MINVALUE | MAXVALUE] < ,...)>
              <INCLUSIVE | EXCLUSIVE>
          EVERY <(>[Constant] <DurationLabel><)>
          )
```

or

```
  PARTITION BY <RANGE>
      ([ColumnName] <NULLS LAST | NULLS FIRST> ,...)
      (<PARTITION [PartitionName]>
       STARTING <FROM>
              <(> [Start | MINVALUE | MAXVALUE] < ,...)>
              <INCLUSIVE | EXCLUSIVE>
          ENDING <AT>
              <(> [End | MINVALUE | MAXVALUE] < ,...)>
              <INCLUSIVE | EXCLUSIVE>
          <IN [TableSpaceName]>
      )
```

where:

ColumnName   Identifies one or more columns, by name, whose values are to be used to determine which data partition a particular row is to be stored in. (The group of columns specified make up the partitioning key for the table.)

PartitionName   Identifies the unique name that is to be assigned to the data partition to be created.

Start   Specifies the low end of the range for each data partition.

End   Specifies the high end of the range for each data partition.

Constant   Specifies the width of each data-partition range when the automatically generated form of the syntax is used. Data partitions will be created starting at the STARTING FROM value and will contain this number of values in the range. This form of the syntax is supported only if the partitioning key is made up of a single column that has been assigned a numeric, date, time, or timestamp data type.

DurationLabel   Identifies the duration that is associated with the *Constant* value specified if the partitioning key column has been assigned a date, time, or timestamp data type. The following values are valid for this parameter: YEAR, YEARS, MONTH, MONTHS, DAY, DAYS, HOUR, HOURS, MINUTE, MINUTES, SECOND, SECONDS, MICROSECOND, and MICROSECONDS.

TableSpaceName Identifies the table space in which each data partition is to be stored.

Thus, if you wanted to create a table named SALES that is partitioned such that each quarter's data is stored in a different data partition, and each partition resides in a different table space, you could do so by executing a CREATE TABLE SQL statement that looks something like this:

```
CREATE TABLE sales
    (sales_date       DATE,
     sales_amt        NUMERIC(5,2))
    IN tbsp0, tbsp1, tbsp2, tbsp3
    PARTITION BY RANGE (sales_date NULLS FIRST)
        (STARTING '1/1/2006' ENDING '12/31/2006'
         EVERY 3 MONTHS)
```

On the other hand, if you wanted to create a table named DEPARTMENTS that is partitioned such that rows with numerical values that fall in the range of 0 to 9 are stored in one partition that resides in one table space, rows with numerical values that fall in the range of 10 to 19 are stored in another partition that resides in another table space, and so on, you could do so by executing a CREATE TABLE SQL statement that looks something like this:

```
CREATE TABLE departments
    (dept_no    INT
     desc       CHAR(3))
    PARTITION BY (dept_no NULLS FIRST)
        (STARTING  0 ENDING  9 IN tbsp0,
         STARTING 10 ENDING 19 IN tbsp1,
         STARTING 20 ENDING 29 IN tbsp2,
         STARTING 30 ENDING 39 IN tbsp3)
```

It is important to note that when an index is created for a range-partitioned table, the data for that index will be stored in the table space that is used to hold the first partition's data, unless otherwise specified.

Data Row Compression

Along with table partitioning and pureXML, one of the most prominent features introduced in DB2 9 is the ability to reduce the amount of storage needed to store table data using what is known as data row compression. Although the primary purpose of data row compression is to save storage space, it can lead to significant disk I/O savings and higher buffer pool hit ratios as well. (More data can be cached in memory.) All of this can lead to an increase in performance, but not without some cost—extra CPU cycles are needed to compress and decompress the data.

Data row compression works by searching for repeating patterns in the data and replacing the patterns with 12-bit symbols, which are stored along with the pattern they represent in a static dictionary. (Once this dictionary is created, it is stored in the table along with the compressed data and is loaded into memory whenever data in the table is accessed to aid in decompression.) This is done by scanning an entire table and looking for repeating column values, as well as repeating patterns that span multiple columns in a row. DB2 also looks for repeating patterns that are substrings of a given column. However, just because a repeating pattern is found does not mean that the data is automatically compressed—data is compressed only where storage savings will be realized. Figure 3–2 illustrates how data row compression works.

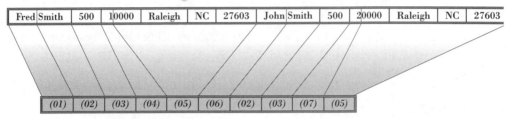

EMPLOYEE TABLE

NAME	DEPT	SALARY	CITY	STATE	ZIPCODE
Fred Smith	500	10000	Raleigh	NC	27603
John Smith	500	20000	Raleigh	NC	27603

UNCOMPRESSED DATA ROWS ON DISK

| Fred | Smith | 500 | 10000 | Raleigh | NC | 27603 | John | Smith | 500 | 20000 | Raleigh | NC | 27603 |

| (01) | (02) | (03) | (04) | (05) | (06) | (02) | (03) | (07) | (05) |

COMPRESSED DATA ROWS ON DISK

COMPRESSION DICTIONARY

SYMBOL	PATTERN
01	Fred
02	Smith
03	500
04	1

Figure 3–2: How data row compression works.

In order to use data row compression with a table, two prerequisites must be satisfied:

1. Compression must be enabled at the table level.

2. A compression dictionary for the table must be built.

Enabling a Table for Data Row Compression

Compression is enabled at the table level by executing either the CREATE TABLE SQL statement or the ALTER TABLE statement with the COMPRESS YES option specified. For example, if you wanted to create a new table named EMPLOYEE and enable it for data row compression, you could do so by executing a CREATE TABLE statement that looks something like this:

```
CREATE TABLE employee
    (name      VARCHAR(60),
     dept      CHAR(3),
     salary    DECIMAL(7,2),
     city      VARCHAR(25),
     state     CHAR(2),
     zipcode   VARCHAR(10))
  COMPRESS YES
```

On the other hand, if you wanted to enable an existing table named EMPLOYEE for data row compression, you could do so by executing an ALTER TABLE statement that looks like this:

```
ALTER TABLE employee COMPRESS YES
```

Building a Compression Dictionary

Although you can enable a table for data row compression at any time by setting its COMPRESS attribute to YES, data stored in the table will not be compressed until a compression dictionary has been built. A compression dictionary is built (and data in a table is compressed) through an offline table reorganization operation; such an operation is initiated by executing the REORG command with either the KEEPDICTIONARY or the RESETDICTIONARY option specified. If the REORG command is executed with either option specified, and a compression dictionary does not exist, a new dictionary will be built; if the REORG command is executed with either option specified, and a dictionary already exists, data in the table will be reorganized/compressed, and the existing dictionary will either be recreated (RESETDICTIONARY) or left as it is (KEEPDICTIONARY).

Thus, if you wanted to create a new compression dictionary (and compress the existing data) for a table named EMPLOYEE that has been enabled for data row compression, you could do so by executing a REORG command that looks like this:

```
REORG TABLE employee RESETDICTIONARY
```

When this command is executed, data stored in the EMPLOYEE table will be analyzed, a compression dictionary will be constructed and stored at the beginning of the table, and the data will be compressed and written to the table directly behind the compression dictionary.

It is important to note that index data is not affected by data row compression; only data stored on a page in a base table can be compressed. However, because records in a compressed table are moved between storage and memory in compressed form (the compression dictionary is moved into memory as well so that decompression can take place), records for compressed tables that are written to transaction log files will be compressed as well.

Estimating Storage Savings from Data Row Compression

Because an offline reorganization operation is needed to construct a compression dictionary and perform data compression, the initial overhead required to compress data can be quite high. Therefore, it can be beneficial to know which tables will benefit the most from data row compression and which tables will not. In DB2 9, the Inspect utility can help you make that determination. The Inspect utility is invoked by executing the INSPECT command, and if this command is executed with the ROWCOMPESTIMATE option specified, the Inspect utility will examine each row in the table specified, build a compression dictionary from the data found, and then use this dictionary to estimate how much space will be saved if the data in the table is compressed.

Thus, if you want to estimate how much storage space will be saved if the data in a table named EMPLOYEE is compressed, you could do so by executing an INSPECT command that looks something like this:

```
INSPECT ROWCOMPESTIMATE TABLE NAME employee
```

Practice Questions

Question 1

> The following command is executed:
>
>   CREATE DATABASE test ON C: USING CODESET UTF-8 TERRITORY US
>
> How many DMS table spaces are created?
>
> ○ A. 0
>
> ○ B. 1
>
> ○ C. 2
>
> ○ D. 3

Question 2

> Which of the following features is NOT automatically enabled when a new DB2 9 database is created?
>
> ○ A. Automatic maintenance
>
> ○ B. Self-tuning memory manager
>
> ○ C. The Health Monitor
>
> ○ D. Data row compression

Question 3

> If the following CREATE DATABASE command is executed:
>
>   CREATE DATABASE sales ON /mnt/data1, /mnt/data2
>   COLLATE USING IDENTITY
>   CATALOG TABLESPACE MANAGED BY SYSTEM USING ('mnt/syscat');
>
> Which of the following statements is NOT true about the resulting database?
>
> ○ A. Automatic storage is enabled for the database
>
> ○ B. An SMS table space will be used to hold the system catalog
>
> ○ C. User data will be stored on /mnt/data1 and /mnt/data2
>
> ○ D. Metadata for the database will be stored on /mnt/data2

Question 4

A database administrator wants to create a DB2 9 database named PAYROLL with automatic storage enabled. The storage containers for the database should reside on /home/data1 and /home/data2; the metadata files for the database should reside on /home/dbase.

Which of the following commands must be executed to accomplish this?

O A. CREATE DB payroll ON /home/dbase DBPATH ON /home/data1, /home/data2

O B. CREATE DB payroll ON /home/dbase AUTOMATIC STORAGE YES USING /home/data1, /home/data2

O C. CREATE DB payroll ON /home/data1, /home/data2 DBPATH ON /home/dbase

O D. CREATE DB payroll ON /home/dbase AUTOMATIC STORAGE ON /home/data1, /home/data2

Question 5

A table space named TBSP1 was created by executing the following command:

```
CREATE TABLESPACE tbsp1
MANAGED BY DATABASE USING (FILE 'C:\tbsp1.dat' 100 M)
```

Which of the following SQL statement(s) must be executed before table space TBSP1 will be allowed to grow automatically up to 1000 MB?

O A. ALTER TABLESPACE tbsp1 AUTORESIZE YES INCREASESIZE 1000 M;

O D. ALTER TABLESPACE tbsp1 AUTORESIZE YES MAXSIZE 1000 M;

O C. DROP TABLESPACE tbsp1;

   CREATE TABLESPACE tbsp1

   MANAGED BY DATABASE USING (FILE 'C:\tbsp1.dat' 1000 M)

   AUTORESIZE YES;

O D. DROP TABLESPACE tbsp1;

   CREATE TABLESPACE tbsp1

   MANAGED BY DATABASE USING (FILE 'C:\tbsp1.dat' 100 M)

   AUTORESIZE YES INCREASESIZE 1000 M;

Question 6

A table space named TBSP1 was created by executing the following command:

```
CREATE REGULAR TABLESPACE tbsp1
MANAGED BY AUTOMATIC STORAGE
```

Which of the following statements is NOT true about table space TBSP1?

○ A. The table space will be created as a DMS table space with file containers.

○ B. The maximum size of the table space will be 2 GB (MAXSIZE 2 G) by default.

○ C. The initial size of the table space could have been specified using the INITIALSIZE option.

○ D. Automatic resizing is on (AUTORESIZE YES) by default.

Question 7

Which of the following statements will create a table named PARTS that is partitioned such that rows with part numbers that fall in the range of 0 to 33 are stored in one partition that resides in one table space, rows with part numbers in the range of 34 to 66 are stored in another partition that resides in another table space, and rows with part numbers in the range of 67 to 99 are stored in a third partition that resides in a third table space?

○ A. CREATE TABLE parts (partno INT, desc VARCHAR(25))
       IN tbsp0, tbsp1, tbsp2
       PARTITION BY (partno NULLS FIRST)
       (STARTING 0 ENDING 33,
       STARTING 34 ENDING 66,
       STARTING 67 ENDING 99)

○ B. CREATE TABLE parts (partno INT, desc VARCHAR(25))
       PARTITION BY (partno NULLS FIRST)
       (PART part0 STARTING 0 ENDING 33,
       PART part1 STARTING 34 ENDING 66,
       PART part2 STARTING 67 ENDING 99)

○ C. CREATE TABLE parts (partno INT, desc VARCHAR(25))
   PARTITION BY (partno NULLS FIRST
   (STARTING 0 ENDING 33,
   STARTING 34 ENDING 66,
   STARTING 67 ENDING 99)
   IN tbsp0, tbsp1, tbsp2)

○ D. CREATE TABLE parts (partno INT, desc VARCHAR(25))
   PARTITION BY (partno NULLS FIRST)
   (STARTING 0 ENDING 33 IN tbsp0,
   STARTING 34 ENDING 66 IN tbsp1,
   STARTING 67 ENDING 99 IN tbsp2)

Question 8

If the following statements are executed in the order shown:

```
CREATE TABLE sales
    (invoice_no      INTEGER,
     sales_date      DATE,
     sales_amt       NUMERIC(5,2))
    IN tbsp0, tbsp1, tbsp2, tbsp3
    PARTITION BY RANGE (sales_date NULLS FIRST)
        (STARTING '1/1/2006' ENDING '12/31/2006'
         EVERY 3 MONTHS);

CREATE INDEX sales_idx ON sales (invoice_no);
```

Which of the following table spaces will contain the data for the SALES_IDX index?

○ A. TBSP0

○ B. TBSP1

○ C. TBSP2

○ D. TBSP3

Question 9

Which two of the following SQL statements must be executed in order to add a new data partition to a range-partitioned table and bring it online?

❑ A. ATTACH PARTITION

❑ B. ALTER TABLE ... ATTACH PARTITION

❑ C. SET INTEGRITY

❑ D. ALTER TABLE ... ENABLE PARTITION

❑ E. ENABLE PARTITION

Question 10

Which of the following is NOT a benefit of table partitioning?

○ A. Enables easy creation of separate ranges of data for subsequent purging or archiving.

○ B. Provides data partition elimination for improved query performance.

○ C. Allows indexes to be placed in different table spaces, allowing for more granular control of index placement.

○ D. Maintains clustering, which reduces the need to reorganize the table.

Question 11

In order to use data row compression with a table, which of the following must exist?

○ A. A compression index

○ B. A compression dictionary

○ C. A user-defined compression algorithm

○ D. A table that only contains character data type columns

Question 12

> Which of the following statements is NOT valid when discussing data row compression?
>
> ○ A. Data row compression can lead to disk I/O savings and improved buffer pool hit ratios.
>
> ○ B. Compressing data at the row level is advantageous because it allows repeating patterns that span multiple columns within a row to be replaced with shorter symbols.
>
> ○ C. Data row compression for a table can be enabled by executing the ALTER TABLE statement with the COMPRESS YES option specified.
>
> ○ D. Only data in a table enabled for data row compression is compressed; data in corresponding indexes and transaction logs is not compressed.

Question 13

> Which two of the following utilities can be used to create a compression dictionary?
>
> ❏ A. reorg
>
> ❏ B. db2pd
>
> ❏ C. inspect
>
> ❏ D. runstats
>
> ❏ E. db2buildcd

Question 14

> Which of the following options can be used with the REORG command to construct a new compression dictionary before compressing data stored in a table?
>
> ○ A. KEEPDICTIONARY
>
> ○ B. RESETDICTIONARY
>
> ○ C. GENERATEDICTIONARY
>
> ○ D. NEWDICTIONARY

Answers

Question 1

The correct answer is **C**. When a new DB2 9 database is created, three table spaces are created and associated with the IBMDEFAULTBP buffer pool. These three table spaces are as follows:

- A regular table space named SYSCATSPACE, which is used to store the system catalog tables and views associated with the database

- A regular table space named USERSPACE1, which is used to store all user-defined objects (such as tables, indexes, and so on) along with user data, index data, and long value data

- A system temporary table space named TEMPSPACE1, which is used as a temporary storage area for operations such as sorting data, reorganizing tables, and creating indexes

Unless otherwise specified, SYSCATSPACE and USERSPACE1 will be DMS File table spaces, and TEMPSPACE1 will be an SMS tables pace; characteristics for each of these table spaces can be provided as input to the CREATE DATABASE command or the Create Database Wizard.

Question 2

The correct answer is **D**. Whenever a new DB2 9 database is created, the following features are enabled by default:

- Automatic maintenance (database backups, table and index reorganization, data access optimization, and statistics profiling).

- Self tuning memory manager (package cache, locking memory, sort memory, database shared memory, and buffer pool memory)

- Utility throttling

- The Health Monitor

Question 3

The correct answer is **D**. The syntax for the CREATE DATABASE command used is this example can be broken down into something that looks like this:

```
CREATE [DATABASE | DB] [DatabaseName]
<AUTOMATIC STORAGE [YES | NO]>
<ON [StoragePath ,...] <DBPATH [DBPath]>>
<COLLATE USING [CollateType]>
<CATALOG TABLESPACE [TS_Definition]>
```

where:

DatabaseName   Identifies the unique name that is to be assigned to the database to be created.

StoragePath   If AUTOMATIC STORAGE YES is specified (the default), identifies one or more storage paths that are to be used to hold table space containers used by automatic storage. Otherwise, identifies the location (drive and/or directory) where the directory hierarchy and files associated with the database to be created are to be physically stored.

DBPath   If AUTOMATIC STORAGE YES is specified (the default), identifies the location (drive and/or directory) where the directory hierarchy and metadata files associated with the database to be created are to be physically stored. (If this parameter is not specified and automatic storage is used, the metadata files will be stored in the first storage path specified in the *StoragePath* parameter.)

CollateType   Specifies the collating sequence (i.e., the sequence in which characters are ordered for the purpose of sorting, merging, and making comparisons) that is to be used by the database to be created. The following values are valid for this parameter: COMPATABILITY, IDENTITY, IDENTITY_16BIT, UCA400_NO, UCA400_LSK, UCA400_LTH, NLSCHAR, and SYSTEM.

TS_Definition   Specifies the definition that is to be used to create the table space that will be used to hold the system catalog tables (SYSCATSPACE).

So in this case, automatic storage is enabled by default, and the storage paths /mnt/data1 and /mnt/data2 will be used to hold table space containers used by automatic storage. And since no database path was specified, the metadata files associated with the database will be stored in the first storage path specified (/mnt/data1).

Question 4

The correct answer is **C**. In this scenario, the syntax for the CREATE DATABASE command is as follows:

```
CREATE [DATABASE | DB] [DatabaseName]
<AUTOMATIC STORAGE [YES | NO]>
<ON [StoragePath ,...] <DBPATH [DBPath]>>
```

where:

DatabaseName   Identifies the unique name that is to be assigned to the database to be created.

StoragePath   If AUTOMATIC STORAGE YES is specified (the default), identifies one or more storage paths that are to be used to hold table space containers used by automatic storage. Otherwise, identifies the location (drive or directory) where the directory hierarchy and files associated with the database to be created are to be physically stored.

DBPath   If AUTOMATIC STORAGE YES is specified (the default), identifies the location (drive or directory) where the directory hierarchy and metadata files associated with the database to be created are to be physically stored. (If this parameter is not specified, and automatic storage is used, the metadata files will be stored in the first storage path specified in the *StoragePath* parameter.)

Because automatic storage is enabled by default when a DB2 9 database is created, the following CREATE DATABASE command will create a database whose storage containers reside on /home/data1 and /home/data2 and whose metadata files reside on /home/dbase:

```
CREATE DB payroll ON /home/data1, /home/data2 DBPATH ON /home/dbase
```

Question 5

The correct answer is **B**. An existing table space's properties can be changed by executing the ALTER TABLESPACE SQL statement. For this scenario, the basic syntax for the ALTER TABLESPACE statement is:

```
ALTER TABLESPACE [TablespaceName]
<AUTORESIZE [NO | YES]>
<INCREASESIZE [IncSize <PERCENT | K | M | G>]>
<MAXSIZE [NONE | MaxSize <K | M | G>]>
```

where:

TablespaceName   Identifies the name assigned to the table space that is to be altered.

IncSize   Identifies the amount by which a table space enabled for automatic resizing will automatically be increased when the table space is full and a request for more space is made.

MaxSize   Identifies the maximum size to which a table space enabled for automatic resizing can automatically be increased.

Thus, if you wanted to change an existing DMS table space named TBSP1 so that it will automatically grow to a maximum size of 1000 MB, you could do so by executing an ALTER TABLESPACE SQL statement that looks like this:

```
ALTER TABLESPACE tbsp1 AUTORESIZE YES MAXSIZE 1000 M
```

Question 6

The correct answer is **B**. Since no maximum size was specified (with the MAXSIZE option of the CREATE TABLESPACE statement), MAXSIZE NONE is used by default and there is no limit on how large the table space can be.

Question 7

The correct answer is **D**. Data from a given table is partitioned into multiple storage objects based on the specifications provided in the PARTITION BY clause of the CREATE TABLE statement. The syntax for this optional clause is:

```
PARTITION BY <RANGE>
  ([ColumnName] <NULLS LAST | NULLS FIRST> ,...)
  (STARTING <FROM>
        <(> [Start | MINVALUE | MAXVALUE] < ,...)>
        <INCLUSIVE | EXCLUSIVE>
    ENDING <AT>
        <(> [End | MINVALUE | MAXVALUE] < ,...)>
```

```
            <INCLUSIVE | EXCLUSIVE>
        EVERY <(>[Constant] <DurationLabel><)>
   )
or

   PARTITION BY <RANGE>
     ([ColumnName] <NULLS LAST | NULLS FIRST> ,...)
     (<PARTITION [PartitionName]>
      STARTING <FROM>
            <(> [Start | MINVALUE | MAXVALUE] < ,...)>
            <INCLUSIVE | EXCLUSIVE>
        ENDING <AT>
            <(> [End | MINVALUE | MAXVALUE] < ,...)>
            <INCLUSIVE | EXCLUSIVE>
        <IN [TableSpaceName]>
   )
```

where:

ColumnName	Identifies one or more columns, by name, whose values are to be used to determine which data partition a particular row is to be stored in. (The group of columns specified make up the partitioning key for the table.)
PartitionName	Identifies the unique name that is to be assigned to the data partition to be created.
Start	Specifies the low end of the range for each data partition.
End	Specifies the high end of the range for each data partition.
Constant	Specifies the width of each data partition range when the automatically generated form of the syntax is used. Data partitions will be created starting at the STARTING FROM value and will contain this number of values in the range. This form of the syntax is only supported if the partitioning key is comprised of a single column that has been assigned a numeric, date, time, or timestamp data type.
DurationLabel	Identifies the duration that is associated with the *Constant* value specified if the partitioning key column has been assigned a date, time, or timestamp data type. The following values are valid for this parameter: YEAR, YEARS, MONTH, MONTHS, DAY, DAYS, HOUR, HOURS, MINUTE, MINUTES, SECOND, SECONDS, MICROSECOND, and MICROSECONDS.
TableSpaceName	Identifies the table space that each data partition is to be stored in.

Thus, if you wanted to create a table named PARTS that is partitioned such that rows with numerical values that fall in the range of 0 to 33 are stored in one partition that resides in one table space, rows with numerical values that fall in the range of 34 to 66 are stored in another partition that resides in another table space, and so on, you could do so by executing a CREATE TABLE SQL statement that looks something like this:

```
CREATE TABLE parts
    (partno   INT,
     desc     VARCHAR(25))
    PARTITION BY (partno NULLS FIRST)
        (STARTING  0 ENDING 33 IN tbsp0,
         STARTING 34 ENDING 66 IN tbsp1,
         STARTING 67 ENDING 99 IN tbsp2)
```

Question 8

The correct answer is **A**. When an index is created for a range partitioned table, the data for that index will be stored in the table space that is used to hold the first partition's data, unless otherwise specified. Since, in the example, the following CREATE INDEX SQL statement was used to create an index for the SALES table:

```
CREATE INDEX sales_idx ON sales (invoice_no);
```

Data for the index named SALES_IDX will be stored in the table space named TBSP0.

Question 9

The correct answers are **B** and **C**. A new range can be easily incorporated into a partitioned table, as an additional data partition by using the ATTACH PARTITION clause of the ALTER TABLE statement; once rolled in, newly attached data partitions are brought online by executing the SET INTEGRITY statement.

Question 10

The correct answer is **D**. Table partitioning improves performance and eliminates the need to create a partitioned database using the Data Partitioning Feature. Other advantages of using table partitioning include: easy roll-in and roll-out of data, easier administration of large tables, flexible index placement, and better query processing.

Question 11

The correct answer is **B**. In order to use data row compression with a table, two prerequisites must be satisfied:

1. Compression must be enabled at the table level.

2. A compression dictionary for the table must be built.

Question 12

The correct answer is **D**. Index data is not affected by data row compression; only data stored on a page in a base table can be compressed. However, because records in a compressed table are moved between storage and memory in compressed form (the compression dictionary is moved into memory as well so decompression can take place), records for compressed tables that are written to transaction log files will be compressed as well.

Question 13

The correct answers are **A** and **C**. Although a table can be enabled for data row compression at any time by setting its COMPRESS attribute to YES, data stored in the table will not be compressed until a compression dictionary has been built. A compression dictionary is built (and data in a table is compressed) by performing an offline table reorganization operation; such an operation is initiated by executing the REORG command with either the KEEPDICTIONARY or the RESETDICTIONARY option specified.

Because an offline reorganization operation is needed to construct a compression dictionary and perform data compression, the initial overhead required to compress data can be quite high. Therefore, it can be beneficial to know which tables will benefit the most from data row compression and which tables will not. In DB2 9, the Inspect utility can help you make that determination. The Inspect utility is invoked by executing the INSPECT command and if this command is executed with the ROWCOMPESTIMATE option specified, the Inspect utility will examine each row in the table specified, build a compression dictionary from the data found, and then use this dictionary to estimate how much space will be saved if the data in the table is compressed.

Question 14

The correct answer is **B**. A compression dictionary is built (and data in a table is compressed) by performing an offline table reorganization operation; such an operation is initiated by executing the REORG command with either the KEEPDICTIONARY or the RESETDICTIONARY option specified. If the REORG command is executed with either option specified and a compression dictionary does not exist, a new dictionary will be built; if the REORG command is executed with either option specified and a dictionary already exists, data in the table will be reorganized/compressed and the existing dictionary will either be recreated (RESETDICTIONARY) or left as it is (KEEPDICTIONARY).

CHAPTER 4

XML Concepts

Thirteen percent (13%) of the DB2 9 for Linux, UNIX, and Windows Database Administration Upgrade exam (Exam 736) is designed to test your knowledge of storing and manipulating XML data in a DB2 9 database. The questions that make up this portion of the exam are intended to evaluate the following:

- Your ability to use the new XML data type

- Your knowledge of basic XQuery fundamentals

- Your ability to create and manage XML indexes

- Your ability to use basic XML functions such as XMLPARSE(), XMLSERIALIZE(), XMLVALIDATE(), and XMLQUERY()

- Your knowledge of how to use DB2's data movement utilities when working with XML data

This chapter is designed to introduce you to XML and the XML functions available, as well as walk you through the construction of simple XQuery expressions. This chapter is also designed to show you how to create XML indexes and to show you how DB2's data movement utilities can be used to work with XML data.

Working with XML Data

DB2 9's pureXML technology unlocks the latent potential of XML by providing simple efficient access to XML with the same levels of security, integrity, and resiliency taken for granted with relational data. DB2's pureXML technology is available as an add-on feature to DB2 Express Edition, DB2 Workgroup Server Edition, and DB2 Enterprise Server Edition; however, it is part of DB2 Express-C, and the use of pureXML is included in the base DB2 Express-C license. With pureXML, XML data is stored in a hierarchical structure that naturally reflects the structure of XML documents. This structure, along with innovative indexing techniques, allows DB2 to efficiently manage XML data while eliminating the complex and time-consuming parsing that is typically required to store XML data in a relational database. However, there are some restrictions when it comes to using pureXML:

- pureXML can be used only with single-partition databases.

- The use of any pureXML feature will prevent future use of the database-partitioning feature (DPF) that is available with DB2 Enterprise Server Edition (ESE).

- pureXML cannot be used with DB2 Data Warehouse Edition (DWE) because DWE uses DB2 ESE and DPF.

In order to make use of the pureXML feature, a database must be created using the UTF-8 codeset. The UTF-8 codeset is specified through the USING CODESET option of the CREATE DATABASE command; to create a database named XML_DB with a UTF-8 code set, you must execute a CREATE DATABASE command that looks something like this:

```
CREATE DATABASE xml_db USING CODESET UTF-8 TERRITORY US
```

The XML Data Type and XML Columns

To support pureXML, a new data type called XML was introduced with DB2 9. This data type is used to define columns that will be used to store XML values. Each XML value stored must be a well-formed XML document; a well-formed XML document looks something like this:

```xml
<?xml version="1.0" encoding="UTF-8" ?>
<customerinfo xmlns="http://crecord.dat" id="1000">
  <name>John Doe</name>
  <addr country="United States">
    <street>25 East Creek Drive</street>
    <city>Raleigh</city>
```

```
      <state-prov>North Carolina</state-prov>
      <zip-pcode>27603</zip-pcode>
   </addr>
   <phone type="work">919-555-1212</phone>
   <email>john.doe@xyz.com</email>
</customerinfo>
```

XML documents begin with an XML declaration; an XML declaration looks something like this:

```
<?xml version="1.0" encoding="UTF-8" ?>
```

or

```
<?xml version="1.0"?>
```

The XML declaration is followed by one or more attributes and elements. All XML elements are enclosed with opening and closing tags; XML elements look something like this:

```
<p>This is a paragraph</p>
<p>This is another paragraph</p>
```

It is important to note that the opening and closing tags used are case sensitive—the tag <Letter> is different from the tag <letter>. Therefore, opening and closing tags must be written with the same case.

XML attributes are normally used to describe XML elements or to provide additional information about an element. Attributes are always contained within the start tag of an element, and attribute values must always be quoted. Here are some examples:

```
<file type="gif">
```

```
<person id="3344">
```

Attributes are handy in HTML, but in XML you should try to avoid them whenever the same information can be expressed using elements. The following examples convey the same information:

```
<person sex="female">
    <firstname>Anna</firstname>
    <lastname>Smith</lastname>
</person>
```

```
<person>
   <sex>female</sex>
   <firstname>Anna</firstname>
   <lastname>Smith</lastname>
</person>
```

In the first example, SEX is an attribute. In the last example SEX is an element.

To create tables with XML columns, you specify columns with the XML data type in the CREATE TABLE statement. (A table can have one or more XML columns.) Like an LOB column, an XML column holds only a descriptor of the column. The data itself is stored separately. Unlike an LOB column, you do not specify a length when you define an XML column. So to create a table named CUSTOMER that contains an XML column named CUSTINFO, you would execute a CREATE TABLE statement that looks something like this:

```
CREATE TABLE customer
      (custid   INTEGER NOT NULL,
       custinfo XML)
```

XML columns have the following restrictions:

- They cannot have a default value specified by the WITH DEFAULT clause; if the column is nullable, the default for the column is NULL.

- They cannot be referenced in CHECK constraints (except for a VALIDATED predicate).

- They cannot be referenced in generated columns.

- They cannot be included in typed tables and typed views.

- They cannot be used in a range-clustered table (RCT).

- They cannot be used in a range-partitioned table.

- They cannot be used in a multidimensional clustering (MDC) table.

- They cannot be added to tables that have Type-1 indexes defined on them (note that Type-1 indexes are deprecated indexes; indexes created since DB2 UDB Version 8.1 are Type-2 indexes).

- They cannot be specified in the select-list of scrollable cursors.

- They cannot be referenced in the triggered action of a CREATE TRIGGER statement.

- They cannot be included as columns of keys, including primary, foreign, and unique keys; dimension keys of multidimensional clustering (MDC) tables; sequence keys of range-clustered tables; distribution keys; and data-partitioning keys.

- They cannot be used in a table with a distribution key.

- They cannot be part of any index except an index over XML data.

- They cause data blocking to be disabled when retrieving XML data.

- They cannot be compressed using data row compression

Manipulating XML Data

Like traditional data, XML documents can be added to a database table, altered, removed, and retrieved using SQL Data Manipulation Language statements (INSERT, UPDATE, DELETE, and SELECT statements). Typically, XML documents (as defined in the XML 1.0 specification) are manipulated by application programs; when DML operations from an application program are performed, IBM recommends that XML data be manipulated through host variables, rather than literals, so that DB2 can use the host variable data type to determine some of the encoding information needed for processing. And although you can manipulate XML data using XML, binary, or character types, IBM recommends that you use XML or binary types to avoid code page conversion issues.

XML data used in an application is often stored in a serialized string format—when this data is inserted into an XML column or when data in an XML column is updated, it must be converted to its XML hierarchical format. If the application data type used is an XML data type, DB2 performs this operation implicitly. However, if the application data type is a character or binary data type, the XMLPARSE() function must be used to explicitly convert the data from its serialized string format to the XML hierarchical format during insert and update operations. A simple INSERT statement that uses the XMLPARSE() function to insert a string value into an XML column named CUSTINFO in a table named CUSTOMERS might look something like this:

```
INSERT INTO customers (custinfo) VALUES
    (XMLPARSE(DOCUMENT '<name>John Doe</name>'
    PRESERVE WHITESPACE))
```

When the Command Line Processor is used to manipulate XML documents stored in XML columns, string data can be directly assigned to XML columns without an explicit call to the XMLPARSE() function when insert, update, and delete operations are performed. For example, let's say you want to add a record containing XML data to a table named CUSTOMER that has the following characteristics:

Column Name	Data Type
CUSTID	INTEGER
INFO	XML

You could do so by executing an INSERT statement from the Command Line Processor that looks like this:

```
INSERT INTO customer VALUES (1000,
'<customerinfo xmlns="http://custrecord.dat" custid="1000">
  <name>John Doe</name>
  <addr country="United States">
    <street>25 East Creek Drive</street>
    <city>Raleigh</city>
    <state-prov>North Carolina</state-prov>
    <zip-pcode>27603</zip-pcode>
  </addr>
  <phone type="work">919-555-1212</phone>
  <email>john.doe@xyz.com</email>
</customerinfo>')
```

And if you wanted to update the XML data portion of this record from the Command Line Processor, you could do so by executing an UPDATE statement that looks something like this:

```
UPDATE customer SET custinfo =
'<customerinfo xmlns="http://custrecord.dat" custid="1000">
  <name>Jane Doe</name>
  <addr countr"y="Canada">
    <street>25 East Creek Drive</street>
    <city>Raleigh</city>
    <state-prov>North Carolina</state-prov>
    <zip-pcode>27603</zip-pcode>
  </addr>
  <phone type="work">919-555-1212</phone>
```

```
    <email>jane.doe@xyz.com</email>
</customerinfo>'
WHERE XMLEXISTS ('declare default element namespace
"http://custrecord.dat";
$info/customerinfo[name/text()="John Doe"]' PASSING custinfo as "info")
```

Finally, if you wanted to delete the record from the CUSTOMER table, you could do so by executing a DELETE statement from the Command Line Processor that looks something like this:

```
DELETE FROM customer
WHERE XMLEXISTS ('declare default element namespace
"http://custrecord.dat";
$info/customerinfo[name/text()="John Doe"]' PASSING custinfo as "info")
```

So how do you retrieve XML data once it has been stored in a table? With DB2 9, XML data can be retrieved using an SQL query or one of the SQL/XML query functions available. When querying XML data using SQL, you can retrieve data only at the column level—in other words, an entire XML document must be retrieved. It is not possible to return fragments of a document using SQL; to query within XML documents, you need to use XQuery.

XQuery is a functional programming language that was designed by the World Wide Web Consortium (W3C) to meet specific requirements for querying XML data. Unlike relational data, which is predictable and has a regular structure, XML data is often unpredictable, highly variable, sparse, and self-describing. Because the structure of XML data is unpredictable, the queries that are performed on XML data often differ from typical relational queries. For example, you might need to create XML queries that perform the following operations:

- Search XML data for objects that are at unknown levels of the hierarchy.

- Perform structural transformations on the data (for example, you might want to invert a hierarchy).

- Return results that have mixed types.

In XQuery, expressions are the main building blocks of a query. Expressions can be nested, and they form the body of a query. A query can also have a prolog that contains a series of declarations that define the processing environment for the query. Thus, if you wanted to retrieve customer names for all customers who reside in North Carolina from XML documents stored in the CUSTINFO column of a table named CUSTOMER (assuming this table has been populated with the INSERT statement we looked at earlier), you could do so by executing an XQuery expression that looks something like this:

```
XQUERY declare default element namespace "http://custrecord.dat"; for
$info in db2-fn:xmlcolumn('CUSTOMER.CUSTINFO')/customerinfo where
$info/addr/state-prov="North Carolina" return $info/name
```

And when this XQuery expression is executed from the Command Line Processor, it should return information that looks like this (again, assuming this table has been populated with the INSERT statement we looked at earlier):

```
1
_____
<name xmlns="http://custrecord.dat">John Doe</name>
```

If you wanted to remove the XML tags and just return the customer name, you could do so by executing an XQuery expression that looks like this instead:

```
XQUERY declare default element namespace "http://custrecord.dat"; for
$info in db2-fn:xmlcolumn('CUSTOMER.CUSTINFO')/customerinfo where
$info/addr/state-prov="North Carolina" return $info/name/text()
```

Now when the XQuery expression is executed from the Command Line Processor, it should return information that looks like this:

```
1
_____
John Doe
```

As mentioned previously, XQuery expressions can be invoked from SQL using any of the following SQL/XML functions or predicates:

> **XMLQUERY().** XMLQUERY() is an SQL scalar function that enables you to execute an XQuery expression from within an SQL context. XMLQUERY() returns an XML value, which is an XML sequence. This sequence can be empty, or it can contain one or more items. You can also pass variables to the XQuery expression specified in XMLQUERY().

XMLTABLE(). XMLTABLE() is an SQL table function that returns a table from the evaluation of XQuery expressions. XQuery expressions normally return values as a sequence; however, XMLTABLE() allows you to execute an XQuery expression and return values as a table instead. The table that is returned can contain columns of any SQL data type, including XML. The structure of the resulting table is defined by the COLUMNS clause of XMLTABLE().

XMLEXISTS. The XMLEXISTS predicate determines whether an XQuery expression returns a sequence of one or more items. If the XQuery expression specified in this predicate returns an empty sequence, XMLEXISTS returns FALSE; otherwise, TRUE is returned. The XMLEXISTS predicate can be used in the WHERE clauses of UPDATE, DELETE, and SELECT statements. This usage means that values from stored XML documents can be used to restrict the set of rows that a DML statement operates on.

Additionally, XML data can be converted to character or BLOB data with the XMLSERIALIZE() function while character or BLOB data can be parsed to yield well-formed XML documents using the XMLPARSE() function.

By executing XQuery expressions from within the SQL context, you can

- operate on parts of stored XML documents, instead of entire XML documents (only XQuery can query within an XML document; SQL alone queries at the whole document level);

- enable XML data to participate in SQL queries;

- operate on both relational and XML data; and

- apply further SQL processing to the returned XML values (for example, ordering results with the ORDER BY clause of a subselect).

Thus, assume you wanted to retrieve customer IDs and customer names for a table named CUSTOMER that has the following characteristics:

Column Name	Data Type
CUSTID	INTEGER
INFO	XML

You could do so (assuming this table has been populated with the INSERT statement we looked at earlier) by executing an SELECT statement from the Command Line Processor that looks something like this:

```
SELECT custid, XMLQUERY ('declare default element namespace
"http://custrecord.dat"; $d/customerinfo/name' passing CUSTINFO as "d")
AS address
FROM customer;
```

And when this query is executed, it should return information that looks something like this:

```
CUSTID ADDRESS
------ ----------------------------------------------------------
  1000 <name xmlns="http://custrecord.dat">John Doe</name>
```

XML Indexes

Just as an index over relational data can be used to improve query performance, an index over XML data can be used to improve the efficiency of queries on XML documents that are stored in an XML column. In contrast to traditional relational indexes, where index keys are composed of one or more columns that you specify, an index over XML data uses a particular XML pattern expression to index paths and values found in XML documents stored in a single column. The data type of that column must be XML.

To identify those parts of the document that will be indexed, an XML pattern is used to specify a set of nodes within the XML document. This pattern expression is similar to the path expression defined in the XQuery language, but it differs in that only a subset of the XQuery language is supported. Path expression steps are separated by the forward slash (/). The double forward slash (//)—which is the abbreviated syntax for /descendant-or-self::node()/—may also be specified. In each step, a forward axis (child::, @, attribute::, descendant::, self::, and descendant-or-self::) is chosen, followed by an XML name test or XML kind test. If no forward axis is specified, the child axis is used as the default. Figure 3–12 shows a simple XML pattern and how it is used to identify a specific value within an XML document.

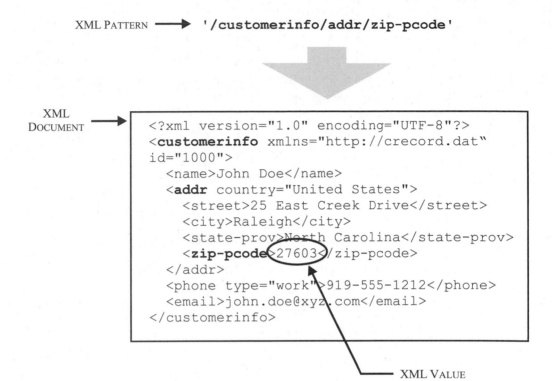

Figure 4–1: How an XML pattern is used to identify a specific value within an XML document.

Instead of providing access to the beginning of a document, index entries in an index over XML data provide access to nodes within the document by creating index keys based on XML pattern expressions. And because multiple parts of an XML document can satisfy an XML pattern, multiple index keys may be inserted into the index for a single document.

XML indexes are created by specifying the GENERATE KEY USING XMLPATTERN clause of the CREATE INDEX SQL statement when an index is created. The basic syntax for this optional clause is:

```
GENERATE KEY USING XMLPATTERN
<Namespace>
[XMLPattern]
AS [SQLDataType]
```

where:

Namespace	Identifies a valid namespace declaration that is used to identify namespace prefixes when qualified names are used in the pattern expression specified.
XMLPattern	Specifies a pattern expression that identifies the nodes that are to be indexed. The pattern expression provided can contain any of the following XQuery components:

- * (asterisk)—Specifies a pattern-matching character.

- / (forward slash)—Separates path expression steps.

- // (double forward slash)—The abbreviated syntax for /descendant-or-self::node()/..

- child::—Specifies children of the context node. This is the default if no other forward axis is specified.

- @—Specifies attributes of the context node. This is the abbreviated syntax for attribute::.

- attribute::—Specifies attributes of the context node.

- descendant::—Specifies the descendants of the context node.

- self::—Specifies just the context node itself.

- descendant-or-self::—Specifies the context node and the descendants of the context node.

SQLDataType	Specifies the SQL data type to which indexed values are converted before they are stored. The following values are valid for this parameter: VARCHAR(*Size*), DOUBLE, DATE, and TIMESTAMP.

Thus, if you wanted to create an XML index using postal/zip code values found in an XML column named CUSTINFO in a table named CUSTOMER and to store those values as DOUBLE values, you could do so by executing a CREATE INDEX statement that looks something like this:

```
CREATE INDEX custindex ON customer(custinfo)
GENERATE KEY
USING XMLPATTERN '/customerinfo/addr/zip-pcode'
AS SQL DOUBLE;
```

On the other hand, if you wanted to create an XML index using address information found in an XML column named CUSTINFO in a table named CUSTOMER and to store those values as VARCHAR values, you could do so by executing a CREATE INDEX statement that looks something like this:

```
CREATE INDEX custindex ON customer(custinfo)
GENERATE KEY
USING XMLPATTERN /customerinfo/@addr'
AS SQL VARCHAR(100);
```

In the first example, the index is created for an element; in the second, it is created for an attribute. Although it is possible to create XML indexes on attributes (or on the entire document, for that matter), performance can suffer. Therefore, it is usually better to create XML indexes on individual elements within an XML document.

DB2's Data Movement Utilities

Although a database usually functions as a self-contained entity, there are times when it becomes necessary to exchange data with "the outside world." That's the purpose of DB2's data movement utilities. For this reason, DB2 provides three different utilities that are designed to move data between databases and external files. These utilities are:

- The Export utility

- The Import utility

- The Load utilityIn

In DB2 9, the Export and Import utilities have been updated to support the native XML data type. The Load utility has not.

The Export Utility

The Export utility is designed to extract data from a DB2 database table or view and externalize it to a file, using the delimited ASCII (DEL) format, the worksheet format (WSF), or the PC Information Exchange Format (IXF) format. Such files can then be used to provide data values to other databases (including the database from which the data was extracted) and software applications such as spreadsheets and word processors.

One way to invoke the Export utility is by executing the EXPORT command. The basic syntax for this command is:

```
EXPORT TO [FileName] OF [DEL | WSF | IXF]
<LOBS TO [LOBPath ,...]>
<LOBFILE [LOBFileName ,...]>
<XML TO [XMLPath ,...]>
<XMLFILE [XMLFileName ,...]>
<MODIFIED BY [Modifier ,...]>
<METHOD N ([ColumnName ,...])>
<MESSAGES [MsgFileName]>
[SELECTStatement | XQueryExpression]
```

where:

FileName   Identifies the name and location of the external file data to which data is to be exported (copied).

LOBPath   Identifies one or more locations where large object (LOB) data values are to be stored. (If this option is specified, each LOB value found will be stored in its own file at the location specified.)

LOBFileName   Identifies one or more base names that are to be used to name the files to which large object (LOB) data values are to be written. During an export operation, file names are constructed by appending a period (.) and a three-digit sequence number to the current base file name in this list, and then appending the generated file name to the large object data path specified (in *LOBPath*). For example, if the current LOB path is the directory "C:\LOBData" and the current LOB file name is "Value," the

LOB files created will be C:\LOBData\Value.001.lob, C:\LOBData\Value.002.lob, and so on.

XMLPath Identifies one or more locations where Extensible Markup Language (XML) documents are to be stored. (If this option is specified, each XML value found will be stored in its own file at the location specified.)

XMLFileName Identifies one or more base names that are to be used to name the files to which Extensible Markup Language (XML) documents are to be written. During an export operation, file names are constructed by appending a period (.) and a three-digit sequence number to the current base file name in this list and then appending the generated file name to the XML data path specified (in *XMLPath*). For example, if the current XML path is the directory "C:\XMLData", and the current XML file name is "Value," the XML files created will be C:\XMLData\Value.001.xml, C:\XMLData\Value.002.xml, and so on.

Modifier Identifies one or more options that are used to override the default behavior of the Export utility. (Table 4.1 contains a list of valid modifiers that can be used when exporting XML data.)

ColumnName Identifies one or more column names that are to be written to the external file to which data is to be exported.

MsgFileName Identifies the name and location of an external file to which messages produced by the Export utility are to be written as the export operation is performed.

SELECTStatement Identifies a SELECT SQL statement that, when executed, will retrieve data that is to be copied to an external file.

XQueryExpression Identifies an XQuery expression that, when executed, will retrieve data that is to be copied to an external file.

Table 4.1 XML-Specific File Type Modifiers Recognized by the EXPORT Command		
Modifier	**Description**	**File Format**
xmlinsepfiles	Indicates that each XML document (XQuery Data Model, or QDM instance) is written to a separate file. By default, multiple values are concatenated together in the same file.	Delimited ASCII (DEL), Worksheet Format (WSF), and PC Integrated Exchange Format (IXF)
xmlnodeclaration	Indicates that XML documents are to be written without an XML declaration tag. By default, XML documents are exported with an XML declaration tag at the beginning that includes an encoding attribute.	Delimited ASCII (DEL), Worksheet Format (WSF), and PC Integrated Exchange Format (IXF)
xmlchar	Indicates that XML documents are to be written using the character code page. (The character code page is the value specified by the *codepage* modifier, or the application code page if this modifier is not specified.) By default, XML documents are written in Unicode.	Delimited ASCII (DEL), Worksheet Format (WSF), and PC Integrated Exchange Format (IXF)
xmlgraphic	Indicates that XML documents are to be encoded and written in the UTF-16 code page, regardless of the application code page or character code page specified with the *codepage* modifier.	Delimited ASCII (DEL), Worksheet Format (WSF), and PC Integrated Exchange Format (IXF)
Adapted from Tables 28, 29, 30, and 31 on pages 821–824 of the *IBM DB2 9 Command Reference* manual.		

So if you wanted to export data stored in a table named DEPARTMENT to a a delimited ASCII (DEL)–format external file named DEPT.DEL, you could do so by executing an EXPORT command that looks something like this:

```
EXPORT TO dept.del OF DEL
MESSAGES exp_msgs.txt
SELECT * FROM department
```

When exporting XML data, all QDM (XQuery Data Model) instances found are written to one or more files that are separate from the main data file containing exported relational data (but in the same location). This is true even if neither the XMLFILE nor the XML TO option is specified. By default, exported QDM instances are concatenated together in a single file; you can use the *xmlinsepfiles* file type modifier to specify that each QDM instance be written to a separate file (which is assigned a name that either you or the Export utility provides). Figure 4–2 illustrates a simple export operation in which XML documents are processed in this manner.

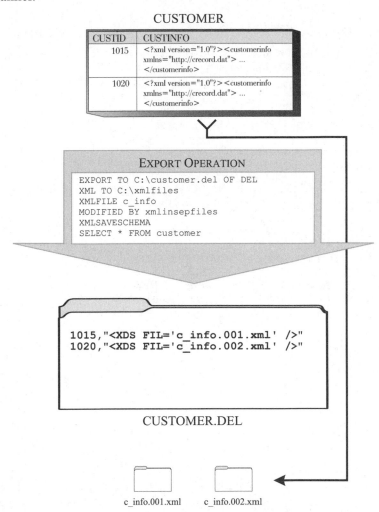

Figure 4–2: An export operation in which XML values are stored in individual files

The Import Utility

Just as there are times when it is beneficial to copy data stored in a table or view to an external file, there can be times when it is advantageous to copy data stored in an external file to a database table or updatable view. One way to copy data from an external file to a database is by using DB2's Import utility; the Import utility is designed to read data directly from an external file (provided the file is written in a format that is supported by DB2) and insert it in a specific table or updatable view.

The Import utility can be invoked by executing the IMPORT command. The basic syntax for this command is:

```
IMPORT FROM [FileName] OF [DEL | ASC | WSF | IXF]
<LOBS FROM [LOBPath ,...]>
<XML FROM [XMLPath ,...]>
<MODIFIED BY [Modifier ,...]>
<Method>
<XML PARSE [STRIP | PRESERVE] WHITESPACE>
<XMLVALIDATE USING [XDS | SCHEMA [SchemaID]]>
<ALLOW NO ACCESS | ALLOW WRITE ACCESS>
<COMMITCOUNT [CommitCount] | COMMITCOUNT AUTOMATIC>
<RESTARTCOUNT | SKIPCOUNT [RestartCount]>
<NOTIMEOUT>
<WARNINGCOUNT [WarningCount]>
<MESSAGES [MsgFileName]>
[CREATE | INSERT | INSERT_UPDATE | REPLACE |
 REPLACE_CREATE]
    INTO [TableName] <([ColumnName ,...])>
    <IN [TSName] <INDEX IN [TSName]> <LONG IN [TSName]>>
```

where:

FileName   Identifies the name and location of the external file from which data is to be imported (copied).

LOBPath   Identifies one or more locations where large object (LOB) data values that are to be imported are stored.

XMLPath   Identifies one or more locations where XML documents that are to be imported are stored.

Modifier   Identifies one or more options that are used to override the default behavior of the Import utility. (Table 4.2 contains a list of valid modifiers that can be used when importing XML data.)

Method   Identifies the method (location, name, or position) that is to be used to extract data values from the source external file(s) specified and map them to one or more columns of the target table/updatable view specified. The syntax used to specify each method varies. (We will look at this syntax a little later.)

SchemaID   Identifies the XML schema/SQL identifier against which XML documents being imported are to be validated. When XML documents are validated in this manner, the SCH attribute of the XML Data Specifier (XDS) is ignored.

CommitCount   Identifies the number of rows of data (records) that are to be copied to the table/updatable view specified before a commit operation is to be performed. (COMMITCOUNT AUTOMATIC should be used instead for import operations that fail because transaction logs become full.)

RestartCount   Identifies the number of rows of data in the external file specified that are to be skipped. This option is typically used when an earlier import operation failed—by skipping rows that have already been successfully imported into a table/updatable view, one import operation can essentially continue where another import operation left off.

WarningCount   Identifies the number of warnings that are allowed before the import operation is to be stopped. (If the file to be imported or the target table is specified incorrectly, the Import utility will generate a warning for each row that it attempts to import.) If this parameter is set to 0 or not specified, the import operation will continue regardless of the number of warnings issued.

MsgFileName   Identifies the name and location of an external file to which messages produced by the Import utility are to be written as the import operation is performed.

TableName   Identifies the name assigned to the table or updatable view to which data is to be imported (copied). (This cannot be the name of a system catalog table or view.)

ColumnName Identifies one or more specific columns (by name) to which data is to be imported.

TSName Identifies the table space in which the table and its regular data, indexes, and/or long data/large object data are to be stored if the table specified is to be created.

Table 4.2 XML-Specific File Type Modifiers Recognized by the IMPORT Command		
Modifier	**Description**	**File Format**
xmlchar	Specifies that XML documents are encoded in the character code page. This modifier is useful for processing XML documents that are encoded in the specified character code page but do not contain an encoding declaration.	Delimited ASCII (DEL) and non-delimited ASCII (ASC)
xmlgraphic	Specifies that XML documents are encoded in the graphic code page specified. This modifier is useful for processing XML documents that are encoded in a specific graphic code page but do not contain an encoding declaration.	Delimited ASCII (DEL) and non-delimited ASCII (ASC)
Adapted from Tables 22, 23, 24, 25, and 26 on pages 810–819 of the *IBM DB2 9 Command Reference* manual.		

Three methods are used to map data values found in external files to columns in a table: the location method, the name method, and the position method. The syntax used to indicate that the location method is to be used to extract data values from the external file specified is:

```
METHOD L ( [ColumnStart] [ColumnEnd] ,... )
    <NULL INDICATORS ( [NullIndColNumber ,...] )>
```

where:

ColumnStart Identifies the starting position of one or more data values in the non-delimited ASCII (ASC) formatted file from which values are to be retrieved.

ColumnEnd   Identifies the ending position of one or more data values in the non-delimited ASCII (ASC) formatted file from which values are to be retrieved.

NullIndColNumber   Identifies the position of one or more data values that are to be treated as null indicator variables for column data values in the non-delimited ASCII (ASC) formatted file from which values are to be retrieved.

The syntax used to indicate that the name method is to be used to extract data values from the external file specified is:

```
METHOD N ( [ColumnName ,...] )
```

where:

ColumnName   Identifies one or more unique names assigned to columns in the PC Integrated Exchange Format (IXF) formatted file from which values are to be retrieved.

And the syntax used to indicate that the position method is to be used to extract data values from the external file specified is:

```
METHOD P ( [ColumnPosition ,...] )
```

where:

ColumnPosition   Identifies the indexed position of one or more columns in the delimited ASCII (DEL) or PC Integrated Exchange Format (IXF) formatted file from which values are to be retrieved.

Thus, if you wanted to import data stored in a PC Integrated Exchange Format (IXF)–format external file named DEPT.IXF to a new table named DEPARTMENT, you could do so by executing an IMPORT command that looks something like this:

```
IMPORT FROM C:\dept.ixf OF IXF
MESSAGES imp_msgs.txt
CREATE INTO department IN hr_space1
```

Earlier, we saw that when data that is to be exported contains XML values, each QDM (XQuery Data Model) instance found can be in its entirety in its own individual file that is assigned a name that either the user or the Export utility provides. XML values that reside in individual files can also be imported if the XML FROM option is used. And because the names and locations of files containing XML data values are stored in the source data file (assuming the source data file was produced by the Export utility) along with other relational data, this information does not have to be provided to the Import utility in order for the XML data values to be retrieved.

db2move and db2look

It's easy to see how the Export utility can be used together with the Import utility to copy a table from one database to another. But what if you want to copy several tables or an entire database? In this case, data can be copied on a table-by-table basis using the Export and Import or Load utilities (if PC Integrated Exchange Format (IXF) formatted files are used, the table structure and any associated indexes will be copied as well), but a more efficient way to copy an entire DB2 database is by using the db2move utility. This utility queries the system catalog tables of the specified database and compiles a list of all user tables found. It then exports the contents and table structure of each table in the database to individual PC Integrated Exchange Format (IXF) formatted files. The set of files produced can then be imported or loaded to another DB2 database on the same system, or they can be transferred to another workstation and be imported or loaded to a DB2 database residing there.

The db2move utility can be run in one of four different modes: EXPORT, IMPORT, LOAD, or COPY. When run in EXPORT mode, db2move invokes the Export utility to extract data from one or more tables and externalize it to PC Integrated Exchange Format (IXF) formatted files. It also produces a file named db2move.lst that contains the names of all tables processed, along with the names of the files to which each table's data was written. Additionally, the db2move utility may also produce one or more message files that contain warning or error messages that were generated as a result of the Export operation.

When run in IMPORT mode, db2move invokes the Import utility to recreate each table and their associated indexes using information stored in PC Integrated Exchange Format (IXF) formatted files. When run in this mode, the file db2move.lst is used to establish a link between the PC Integrated Exchange Format (IXF) formatted files needed and the tables into which data is to be imported.

When run in LOAD mode, db2move invokes the Load utility to populate tables that already exist with data stored in PC Integrated Exchange Format (IXF) formatted files. Again, the file db2move.lst is used to establish a link between the PC Integrated Exchange Format (IXF) formatted files needed and the tables into which data is to be loaded.

Unfortunately, the db2move utility can be used to migrate only table and index objects. If the database to be migrated contains other objects such as aliases, views, triggers, user-defined data types (UDTs), user-defined functions (UDFs), and so on, you must to duplicate those objects in the target database as well if you want to have an identical copy of the source database. That is where the db2look utility comes in. When invoked, db2look can reverse-engineer an existing database and produce a set of Data Definition Language (DDL) SQL statements, which can then be used to recreate all of the data objects found in the database that was analyzed. The basic syntax for the db2look command is:

```
db2look -d [DatabaseAlias]
<-e>
<-u [Creator]>
<-z [Schema]>
<-t [TableName, ...]>
<-ct>
<-v [ViewName, ...]>
<-o [FileName]>
<-a>
<-x>
<-xd>
<-f>
<-xs <-xdir [Directory]>>
<-h>
```

where:

DatabaseAlias   Identifies the alias assigned to the database that DDL statements are to be generated for.

Creator   Identifies the creator ID that is to be used to limit DDL output. DDL output will be limited to objects that were created by this ID.

Schema   Identifies the schema that is to be used to limit DDL output. DDL output will be limited to objects that reside in this schema.

TableName   Identifies one or more tables, by name, for which DDL statements are to be generated.

ViewName   Identifies one or more views, by name, for which DDL statements are to be generated.

FileName   Identifies, by name, a file that all DDL output produced is to be written to.

Directory   Identifies the location where XML-related files are to be written to. If this option is not specified, all XML-related files will be exported into the current directory.

All other options shown with this command are described in Table 4.3.

Table 4.3 db2look Command Options	
Option	**Meaning**
-e	Indicates that DDL statements are to be extracted for the following database objects: tables, views, materialized query tables (MQTs), aliases, indexes, triggers, sequences, user-defined distinct types, select constraints (primary key, referential integrity, and check constraints), user-defined structured types, user-defined functions, user-defined methods, user-defined transforms, wrappers, servers, user mappings, nicknames, type mappings, function templates, function mappings, index specifications, and stored procedures.
-ct	Indicates that DDL statements are to be generated by object creation time.
-a	Indicates that DDL statements are to be generated for all objects, including inoperative objects, regardless of who created them.
-x	Indicates that authorization DDL statements (GRANT, REVOKE) are to be generated.
-xd	Indicates that all authorization DDL statements, including authorization DDL statements for objects whose authorizations were granted by SYSIBM at object creation time, are to be generated.
-f	Indicates that commands needed to set configuration parameters and registry variables that affect the query optimizer are to be generated.
-xs	Indicates that all files necessary to register XML schemas and Document Type Definitions (DTDs) at the target database are to be exported and appropriate commands for registering them are to be generated.
-h	Displays help information. When this option is specified, all other options are ignored, and only the help information is displayed.

Thus, if you wanted to export all files needed to register XML schemas and DTDs at another database, using XML information stored in a database named EMPLOYEE, you could do so by executing a db2look command that looks something like this:

```
db2look –d employee –a –e –xs –xdir C:\xml_info
```

Practice Questions

Question 1

Which of the following commands will create a database named HR_RECORDS that can be used to store XML data?

○ A. CREATE DATABASE hr_records USING CODESET UTF-8 TERRITORY US

○ B. CREATE DATABASE hr_records XML SUPPORT YES

○ C. CREATE DATABASE hr_records USING CODESET IBM-850 TERRITORY US

○ D. CREATE DATABASE hr_records FOR PUREXML

Question 2

Which of the following SQL statements will create a table named TAB1 with an XML data type column?

○ A. CREATE TABLE tab1 (c1 INT NOT NULL PRIMARY KEY, c2 XML(1000))

○ B. CREATE TABLE tab1 (c1 XML NOT NULL PRIMARY KEY, c2 INT)

○ C. CREATE TABLE tab1 (c1 INT NOT NULL PRIMARY KEY, c2 XML)

○ D. CREATE TABLE tab1 (c1 INT NOT NULL PRIMARY KEY, c2 XML WITH DEFAULT)

Question 3

Which of the following statements about XML indexes is true?

○ A. XML indexes can contain relational data columns.

○ B. An index over XML data can be used to improve the efficiency of XQuery expressions performed against XML columns.

○ C. Unique XML indexes can be created by combining multiple XML columns.

○ D. The entire contents of an XML document stored in an XML column are indexed.

Question 4

If the following CREATE INDEX statements are executed:

```
CREATE INDEX cust_zip_idx ON customer(custinfo)
GENERATE KEY
USING XMLPATTERN '/customerinfo/addr/zip-pcode'
AS SQL DOUBLE;

CREATE INDEX cust_city_idx ON customer(custinfo)
GENERATE KEY
USING XMLPATTERN '/customerinfo/addr/city'
AS SQL VARCHAR(40);
```

And the following XML documents are inserted into the CUSTOMER table:

```
<?xml version="1.0" encoding="UTF-8" ?>
   <customerinfo xmlns="http://crecord.dat" id="1000">
    <name>John Doe</name>
    <addr country="United States">
     <street>25 East Creek Drive</street>
     <city>Raleigh</city>
     <state-prov>North Carolina</state-prov>
     <zip-pcode>27603</zip-pcode>
    </addr>
    <phone type="work">919-555-1212</phone>
    <email>john.doe@yahoo.com</email>
   </customerinfo>

<?xml version="1.0" encoding="UTF-8" ?>
   <customerinfo xmlns="http://crecord.dat" id="1010">
    <name>Jane Smith</name>
    <addr country="United States">
     <street>2120 Stewart Street</street>
     <city></city>
     <state-prov>South Carolina</state-prov>
     <zip-pcode>29501</zip-pcode>
    </addr>
    <phone type="work">843-555-3434</phone>
    <email>jane.smith@aol.com</email>
   </customerinfo>
```

How many index keys will be generated?

○ A. 1

○ B. 2

○ C. 3

○ D. 4

Question 5

What is the purpose of the XMLPARSE() function?

○ A. To convert a well-formed XML document into a character string.

○ B. To support conversions between non-XML data types and the XML data type.

○ C. To convert a character string value into a well-formed XML document.

○ D. To convert a character string value to an XML value with a single XQuery text node.

Question 6

What is the purpose of the XMLSERIALIZE() function?

○ A. To convert a well-formed XML document into a character string.

○ B. To support conversions between non-XML data types and the XML data type.

○ C. To convert a character string value into a well-formed XML document.

○ D. To convert a character string value to an XML value with a single XQuery text node.

Question 7

Which statement about exporting XML data is NOT correct?

○ A. When exporting XML data, the default behavior of the Export utility can be modified using the xmlinsepfiles, xmlnodeclaration, xmlchar, and xmlgraphic file type modifiers.

○ B. If neither the XMLFILE nor the XML TO option is specified with the EXPORT command, XML data will be written to the same file as relational data.

○ C. By default, exported XML files are written to the same path as the exported data file.

○ D. XML data to be exported can be retrieved by invoking an XQuery expression from an SQL query.

Question 8

Which two of the following options can be used with db2look to control how XML data is exported?

❑ A. -x

❑ B. -xs

❑ C. -xdir

❑ D. -xpath

❑ E. -xfname

Answers

Question 1

The correct answer is **A**. In order to make use of the pureXML feature, a database must be created using the UTF-8 codeset. The UTF-8 codeset is specified through the USING CODESET option of the CREATE DATABASE command; to create a database named XML_DB with a UTF-8 code set, you would execute a CREATE DATABASE command that looks something like this:

```
CREATE DATABASE xml_db USING CODESET UTF-8 TERRITORY US
```

Question 2

The correct answer is **C**. To create tables with XML columns, you specify columns with the XML data type in the CREATE TABLE statement. (A table can have one or more XML columns.) Like an LOB column, an XML column holds only a descriptor of the column. The data itself is stored separately. Unlike an LOB column, you do not specify a length when you define an XML column. So to create a table named TAB1 that contains an XML column named C2, you would execute a CREATE TABLE statement that looks like this:

```
CREATE TABLE tab1
    (c1   INTEGER NOT NULL,
     c2   XML)
```

When included in a table definition, XML columns have the following restrictions:

- They cannot have a default value specified by the WITH DEFAULT clause.

- They cannot be referenced in CHECK constraints (except for a VALIDATED predicate).

- They cannot be referenced in generated columns.

- They cannot be included as columns of keys, including primary, foreign, and unique keys; dimension keys of multidimensional clustering (MDC) tables; sequence keys of range-clustered tables; distribution keys; and data-partitioning keys.

- They cannot be used in a table that has a distribution key

Question 3

The correct answer is **B**. Just as an index over relational data can be used to improve query performance, an index over XML data can be used to improve the efficiency of queries on XML documents that are stored in an XML column. In contrast to traditional relational indexes, where index keys are composed of one or more columns you specify, an index over XML data uses a particular XML pattern expression to index paths and values found in XML documents stored in a single column—the data type of that column must be XML. All or part of the contents of an XML column can be indexed.

Question 4

The correct answer is **C**. When the documents specified are inserted into the CUSTINFO column of the CUSTOMER table, the values 27603 and 29501 will be added to the CUST_ZIP_IDX index and the value "Raleigh" will be added to the CUST_CITY_IDX index.

Question 5

The correct answer is **C**. The XMLPARSE() function is designed to convert a character string value into a well-formed XML document. The XMLSERIALIZE() function is designed to convert a well-formed XML document into a character string; the XMLCAST() function is designed to support conversions between non-XML data types and the XML data type; and the XMLTEXT() function is designed to convert a character string value to an XML value with a single XQuery text node.

Question 6

The correct answer is **A**. The XMLSERIALIZE() function is designed to convert a well-formed XML document into a character string. The XMLCAST() function is designed to support conversions between non-XML data types and the XML data type; the XMLPARSE() function is designed to convert a character string value into a well-formed XML document; and the XMLTEXT() function is designed to convert a character string value to an XML value with a single XQuery text node.

Question 7

The correct answer is **B**. When exporting XML data, all QDM (XQuery Data Model) instances found are written to one or more files that are separate from the main data file containing exported relational data (but in the same location). This is true even if neither the XMLFILE nor the XML TO option is specified. By default, exported QDM instances are concatenated together in a single file; you can use the *xmlinsepfiles* file type modifier to specify that each QDM instance be written to a separate file (which is assigned a name that either you or the Export utility provides).

Question 8

The correct answers are **B** and **C**. The –xs option of the db2look command is used to indicate that all files necessary to register XML schemas and Document Type Definitions (DTDs) at the target database are to be exported and appropriate commands for registering them are to be generated. The –xdir [*DirectoryName*] option is used to identify the location where XML-related files are to be written to. If this option is not specified, all XML-related files will be exported into the current directory.

CHAPTER 5

Analyzing DB2 Activity

Sixteen percent (16%) of the DB2 9 for Linux, UNIX, and Windows Database Administration Upgrade exam (Exam 736) is designed to test your ability to use the database monitoring tools that are available with DB2. The questions that make up this portion of the exam are intended to evaluate the following:

- Your ability to use the snapshot monitor functions and administrative routines available with DB2 9

- Your ability to monitor deadlocks

- Your ability to use the troubleshooting utilities available with DB2 9

This chapter is designed to introduce you to the set of monitoring tools that are available with DB2 and to show you how each is used to monitor how well (or how poorly) your database system is operating. This chapter is also designed to introduce you to some of the troubleshooting utilities available with DB2 9.

The Database System Monitor

Database monitoring is a vital activity that, when performed on a regular basis, provides continuous feedback on the health of a database system. And because database monitoring is such an integral part of database administration, DB2 comes equipped with a built-in monitoring utility known as the Database System Monitor. Although the name "Database System Monitor" suggests that only one monitoring tool is available, in reality the Database System Monitor is composed of two distinct tools (a snapshot monitor and one or more event monitors) that can be used to capture and return system monitor information. The snapshot monitor allows you to capture a picture of the state of a database (along with all database activity) at a specific point in time whereas event monitors capture and log data as specific database events occur. Information collected by both tools is stored in entities that are referred to as *monitor elements* (or data elements), and each monitor element used is (1) identified by a unique name and (2) designed to store a certain type of information.

The Database System Monitor employs several methods for presenting the data collected. For both snapshot and event monitors, you have the option of storing all collected data in files or database tables, viewing it on screen, or processing it using a custom application.

The Snapshot Monitor

The snapshot monitor is designed to collect information about the state of a DB2 instance and the databases it controls at a specific point in time (i.e., at the time the snapshot is taken). Additionally, the snapshot monitor can be tailored to retrieve specific types of monitoring data (for example, it could be configured to collect just information about buffer pools). Snapshots are useful for determining the status of a database system and, when taken at regular intervals, can provide valuable information that can be used to observe trends and identify potential problem areas.

Snapshot monitor switches

Often, the collection of database system monitor data introduces additional processing overhead. For example, in order to calculate the execution time of SQL statements, the DB2 Database Manager must make a call to the operating system to obtain timestamps before and after every SQL statement is executed; these types of system calls are normally expensive. Another side effect of using the database system monitor is an increase in memory consumption—the DB2 Database Manager uses memory to store data collected for every monitor element tracked.

To help minimize the overhead involved in collecting database system monitor information, a group of switches known as the snapshot monitor switches can be

used to control what information is collected when a snapshot is taken; the type
and amount of information collected is determined by the way these snapshot
monitor switches have been set. Each snapshot monitor switch has two settings: ON
and OFF. When a snapshot monitor switch is set to OFF, monitor elements that fall
under that switch's control do not collect information. The opposite is true if the
switch is set to ON. (Keep in mind that a considerable amount of monitoring
information is not under switch control and will always be collected regardless of
how the snapshot monitor switches have been set.) The snapshot monitor switches
available, along with a description of the type of information that is collected when
each has been set to ON, can be seen in Table 5.1.

Table 5.1 Snapshot Monitor Switches			
Monitor Group	**Monitor Switch**	**DB2 Database Manager Configuration Parameter**	**Information Provided**
Buffer Pools	BUFFERPOOL	*dft_mon_bufferpool*	Amount of buffer pool activity (i.e., number of read and write operations performed and the amount of time taken, for each read/write operation)
Locks	LOCK	*dft_mon_lock*	Number of locks held and number of deadlock cycles encountered
Sorts	SORT	*dft_mon_sort*	Number of sort operations performed, number of heaps used, number of overflows encountered, and the amount of time taken for each sort operation performed
SQL Statements	STATEMENT	*dft_mon_stmt*	SQL statement processing start time, SQL statement processing end time, and SQL statement identification
Tables	TABLE	*dft_mon_table*	Amount of table activity performed, such as number of rows read, number of rows written, and so on
Timestamps	TIMESTAMP	*dft_mon_timestamp*	Times and timestamp information
Transactions (units of work)	UOW	*dft_mon_uow*	Transaction start times, transaction completion times, and transaction completion status
Adapted from Table 2 on page 14 of the *DB2 System Monitor Guide and Reference* manual			

By default, all of the switches shown in Table 5.1 are set to OFF, with the exception
of the TIMESTAMP switch, which is set to ON.

Capturing snapshot data

As soon as a database is activated or a connection to a database is established, the snapshot monitor begins collecting monitor data. However, before the data collected can be viewed, a snapshot must be taken. Snapshots can be taken by executing the GET SNAPSHOT command. The basic syntax for this command is:

```
GET SNAPSHOT FOR
[[DATABASE MANAGER | DB MANAGER | DBM] |
 ALL <DCS> DATABASES |
 ALL <DCS> APPLICATIONS |
 ALL BUFFERPOOLS |
 ALL REMOTE_DATABASES |
 ALL REMOTE_APPLICATIONS |
 ALL ON [DatabaseAlias] |
 <DCS> [DATABASE | DB] ON [DatabaseAlias] |
 <DCS> APPLICATIONS ON [DatabaseAlias] |
 <DCS> APPLICATION [APPLID AppID | AGENTID AgentID] |
 TABLES ON [DatabaseAlias] |
 TABLESPACES ON [DatabaseAlias] |
 LOCKS ON [DatabaseAlias] |
 BUFFERPOOLS ON [DatabaseAlias] |
 REMOTE DATABASES ON [DatabaseAlias] |
 REMOTE APPLICATIONS ON [DatabaseAlias]
 DYNAMIC SQL ON [DatabaseAlias] <WRITE TO FILE>]
```

where:

DatabaseAlias Identifies the alias assigned to the database that snapshot monitor information is to be collected for.

AppID Identifies the application, by ID, for which snapshot monitor information is to be collected.

AgentID Identifies the application, by application handle, for which snapshot monitor information is to be collected for.

So if you wanted to take a snapshot that contained only data collected on locks being held by applications interacting with a database named SAMPLE, you could do so by executing a GET SNAPSHOT command that looks like this:

```
GET SNAPSHOT FOR LOCKS ON sample
```

It is important to keep in mind that the snapshot monitor switches, together with the options available with the GET SNAPSHOT command, determine the type and volume of data that will be returned when a snapshot is taken. If a particular snapshot monitor switch has not been turned on, and a snapshot of the monitoring data that is associated with that switch is taken, the monitoring data captured may not contain any values at all.

Capturing snapshot monitor data using SQL

With earlier versions of DB2, the only way to capture snapshot monitor data was by executing the GET SNAPSHOT command or by calling its corresponding API from an application program. With DB2 UDB version 8.1, the ability to capture snapshot monitor data by constructing a query that referenced one of 20 snapshot monitor table functions available was introduced. Although these functions are still available and can be used in DB2 9, they have been depreciated. Now snapshot monitor data can be obtained by querying special administrative views or by using a new set of SQL table functions. These views and functions are described in detail in Table 5.2.

Administrative View	Table Function	Description
Table 5.2 DB2 9 Snapshot Monitor Administrative Tables and SQL Table Functions		
SYSIBMADM. APPLICATIONS	N/A	This administrative view contains information about connected database applications.
SYSIBMADM. APPL_PERFORMANCE	N/A	This administrative view contains information about the rate of rows selected versus rows read per application.
SYSIBMADM. BP_HITRATIO	N/A	This administrative view contains buffer pool hit ratios, including total, data, and index data.
SYSIBMADM. BP_READ_IO	N/A	This administrative view contains buffer pool read performance information.
SYSIBMADM. BP_WRITE_IO	N/A	This administrative view contains buffer pool write performance information.
SYSIBMADM. CONTAINER_UTILIZATION	N/A	This administrative view contains information about table space containers and utilization rates.
SYSIBMADM. LOCKS_HELD	N/A	This administrative view contains information on current locks held.
SYSIBMADM.LOCKWAITS	N/A	This administrative view contains information on locks that are waiting to be granted.
SYSIBMADM. LOG_UTILIZATION	N/A	This administrative view contains information about log utilization for the currently connected database.
SYSIBMADM.LONG_ RUNNING_SQL	N/A	This administrative view contains information about the longest-running SQL statements in the currently connected database.
SYSIBMADM. QUERY_PREP_COST	N/A	This administrative view contains a list of SQL statements, along with information about the time required to prepare each statement.
SYSIBMADM. SNAPAGENT	SNAP_GET_AGENT()	The administrative view and table function returns information about agents from an application snapshot—in particular, the agent logical data group.
SYSIBMADM. SNAPAGENT_MEMORY_POOL	SNAP_GET_AGENT_ MEMORY_POOL()	This administrative view and table function returns information about memory usage at the agent level.
SYSIBMADM.SNAPAPPL	SNAP_GET_APPL()	This administrative view and table function returns information about applications from an application snapshot—in particular, the appl logical data group.

Table 5.2 DB2 9 Snapshot Monitor Administrative Tables and SQL Table Functions (continued)

Administrative View	Table Function	Description
SYSIBMADM. SNAPAPPL_INFO	SNAP_GET_APPL_ INFO()	This administrative view and table function returns information about applications from an application snapshot—in particular, the appl_info logical data group.
SYSIBMADM.SNAPBP	SNAP_GET_BP()	This administrative view and table function returns information about buffer pools from a bufferpool snapshot—in particular, the bufferpool logical data group.
SYSIBMADM. SNAPBP_PART	SNAP_GET_BP_ PART()	This administrative view and table function returns information about buffer pools from a bufferpool snapshot—in particular, the bufferpool_nodeinfo logical data group.
SYSIBMADM. SNAPCONTAINER	SNAP_GET_ CONTAINER_V91()	This administrative view and table function returns table space snapshot information from the tablespace_container logical data group.
SYSIBMADM. SNAPDB	SNAP_GET_DB_ V91()	This administrative view and table function returns snapshot information from the database (dbase) and database storage (db_storage_group) logical groupings.
SYSIBMADM. SNAPDB_MEMORY_POOL	SNAP_GET_DB_ MEMORY_POOL()	This administrative view and table function returns information about memory usage at the database level for UNIX(R) platforms only.
SYSIBMADM.SNAPDBM	SNAP_GET_DBM()	This administrative view and table function returns the snapshot monitor DB2 database manager (dbm) logical grouping information.
SYSIBMADM. SNAPDBM_MEMORY_POOL	SNAP_GET_DBM_ MEMORY_POOL()	This administrative view and table function returns information about memory usage at the database manager level.
SYSIBMADM. SNAPDETAILLOG	SNAP_GET_ DETAILLOG_V91()	This administrative view and table function returns snapshot information from the detail_log logical data group.
SYSIBMADM. SNAPDYN_SQL	SNAP_GET_DYN_ SQL_V91()	This administrative view and table function returns snapshot information from the dynsql logical data group.
SYSIBMADM.SNAPFCM	SNAP_GET_FCM()	This administrative view and table function returns information about the fast communication manager (FCM) from a database manager snapshot—in particular, the fcm logical data group.

Table 5.2 DB2 9 Snapshot Monitor Administrative Tables and SQL Table Functions (continued)

Administrative View	Table Function	Description
SYSIBMADM. SNAPFCM_PART	SNAP_GET_FCM_ PART()	This administrative view and table function returns information about the fast communication manager (FCM) from a database manager snapshot—in particular, the fcm_node logical data group.
SYSIBMADM.SNAPHADR	SNAP_GET_HADR()	This administrative view and table function returns information about high availability disaster recovery (HADR) from a database snapshot—in particular, the HADR logical data group.
SYSIBMADM.SNAPLOCK	SNAP_GET_LOCK()	This administrative view and table function returns snapshot information about locks—in particular, the lock logical data group.
SYSIBMADM.SNAPLOCKWAIT	SNAP_GET_ LOCKWAIT()	This administrative view and table function returns snapshot information about lock waits—in particular, the lockwait logical data group.
SYSIBMADM.SNAPSTMT	SNAP_GET_STMT()	This administrative view and table function returns information about statements from an application snapshot.
SYSIBMADM. SNAPSTORAGE_PATHS	SNAP_GET_ STORAGE_PATHS()	This administrative view and table function returns a list of automatic storage paths for the database, including file system information for each storage path—specifically, from the db_storage_group logical data group.
SYSIBMADM. SNAPSUBSECTION	SNAP_GET_ SUBSECTION()	This administrative view and table function returns information about application subsections, namely the subsection logical monitor grouping.
SYSIBMADM. SNAPSWITCHES	SNAP_GET_ SWITCHES()	This administrative view and table function returns information about the database snapshot switch state.
SYSIBMADM.SNAPTAB	SNAP_GET_TAB_V9 1()	This administrative view and table function returns snapshot information from the table logical data group.
SYSIBMADM. SNAPTAB_REORG	SNAP_GET_TAB_ REORG()	This administrative view and table function returns table reorganization information.
SYSIBMADM.SNAPTBSP	SNAP_GET_TBSP_ V91()	This administrative view and table function returns snapshot information from the table space logical data group.
SYSIBMADM. SNAPTBSP_PART	SNAP_GET_TBSP_ PART_V91()	This administrative view and table function returns snapshot information from the tablespace_nodeinfo logical data group.

Table 5.2 DB2 9 Snapshot Monitor Administrative Tables and SQL Table Functions (continued)		
Administrative View	Table Function	Description
SYSIBMADM. SNAPTBSP_QUIESCER	SNAP_GET_TBSP_ QUIESCER()	This administrative view and table function returns information about quiescers from a table space snapshot.
SYSIBMADM. SNAPTBSP_RANGE	SNAP_GET_TBSP_ RANGE()	This administrative view and table function returns information from a range snapshot.
SYSIBMADM.SNAPUTIL	SNAP_GET_UTIL()	This administrative view and table function returns snapshot information on utilities from the utility_info logical data group.
SYSIBMADM. SNAPUTIL_PROGRESS	SNAP_GET_UTIL_ PROGRESS()	This administrative view and table function returns information about utility progress—in particular, the progress logical data group.
SYSIBMADM. TBSP_UTILIZATION	N/A	This administrative view contains table space configuration and utilization information.
SYSIBMADM. TOP_DYNAMIC_SQL	N/A	This administrative view contains the top dynamic SQL statements, sortable by number of executions, average execution time, number of sorts, or sorts per statement.

Thus, if you wanted to obtain snapshot monitor lock information for the currently connected database, you could do so by executing a query that looks something like this:

```
SELECT AGENT_ID, LOCK_OBJECT_TYPE, LOCK_MODE, LOCK_STATUS
FROM SYSIBMADM.SNAPLOCK
```

Each DB2 9 snapshot monitor table function available returns the same information as the corresponding administrative view, but the function allows you to retrieve information for a specific database instead of the current connected database. The syntax used to construct a query that references a non-Database Manager–level DB2 9 snapshot monitor table function looks something like this:

```
SELECT * FROM TABLE ([FunctionName]
('[DBName]', [PartitionNum]) AS
[CorrelationName]
```

where:

FunctionName	Identifies the snapshot monitor table function to be used (i.e., one of the functions listed in Table 5.2).
DBName	Identifies the database for which snapshot monitor data is to be collected.
PartitionNum	Identifies the database partition for which snapshot monitor data is to be collected.
CorrelationName	Identifies the name that is to be assigned to the result data set produced by the query.

The syntax used to construct a query that references a Database Manager-level snapshot monitor table function is identical, with one exception: the *DBName* parameter is not used.

In either case, if you wanted to capture snapshot monitor data for the current partition in a partitioned database environment, you could do so by specifying the value -1 for the *PartitionNum* parameter; if you wanted to capture snapshot monitor data for all partitions, you specify the value -2. Similarly, if you wanted to capture snapshot monitor data for the current connected database, you could do so by specifying a null value for the *DBName* parameter, either by using empty single quotation marks (' ') or by using a cast operation to produce a null character value—for example, CAST (NULL AS CHAR).

Thus, if you wanted to obtain snapshot monitor lock information for a database named SAMPLE using the SNAP_GET_LOCK() table function (instead of querying the SYSIBMADM.SNAPLOCK administrative view), you could do so by constructing a query that looks something like this:

```
SELECT AGENT_ID, LOCK_OBJECT_TYPE, LOCK_MODE, LOCK_STATUS
FROM TABLE(SNAP_GET_LOCK('sample',-1)) AS snap_info
```

A word about the SNAP_WRITE_FILE() stored procedure

One of the drawbacks of using the special administrative views or SQL table functions to view snapshot monitor data is that users who do not have SYSADM, SYSCTRL, SYSMAINT, or SYSMON authority, are prevented from accessing the data collected. To get around this problem, a special stored procedure called the SNAP_WRITE_FILE() procedure can be used to capture snapshots of monitor data and save the information collected to files on the database server. Once the snapshot data has been saved to a file, any user can issue queries with the corresponding snapshot table functions, specifying (NULL, NULL) as input values for database-level table functions, and (NULL) for database manager level table functions. The monitor data they receive is pulled from the files generated by the SNAP_WRITE_FILE() stored procedure.

The syntax used to invoke the SNAP_WRITE_FILE() stored procedure is:

```
SNAP_WRITE_FILE([RequestType], [DBName], [PartitionNum])
```

where:

RequestType Identifies a specific snapshot request type, which is used to determine the scope of monitor data that is to be collected. The following values are valid for this parameter: APPL_ALL, BUFFERPOOLS_ALL, DB2, DBASE_ALL, DBASE_LOCKS, DBASE_TABLES, DBASE_TABLESPACES, and DYNAMIC_SQL.

DBName Identifies the database for which snapshot monitor data is to be collected.

PartitionNum Identifies the database partition for which snapshot monitor data is to be collected.

Thus, if you wanted to collect snapshot monitor information on the DB2 Database Manager (defaulting to the currently connected database and current database partition) using the SNAP_WRITE_FILE() stored procedure, you could do so by executing a CALL statement that looks like this:

```
CALL SYSPROC.SNAP_WRITE_FILE ('DB2', '', -1)
```

Once this statement is executed, you can retrieve and display the snapshot data collected by executing a query that looks something like this:

```
SELECT SNAPSHOT_TIMESTAMP,DB2_STATUS FROM TABLE(SNAP_GET_DBM()) AS
snap_info
```

Event Monitors

Whereas the snapshot monitor provides a method for recording information about the state of database activity at a given point in time, an event monitor can be used to record information about database activity *when an event or transition occurs*. Therefore, event monitors provide a way to collect monitor data when events or activities that cannot be monitored using the snapshot monitor occur. For example, suppose you want to capture monitor data whenever a deadlock cycle occurs. If you are familiar with the concept of deadlocks, you may recall that a special process known as the deadlock detector runs quietly in the background and "wakes up" at predefined intervals to scan the locking system in search of a deadlock cycle. If a deadlock cycle exists, the deadlock detector randomly selects one of the transactions involved in the cycle to roll back and terminate. (The transaction that is rolled back and terminated receives an SQL error code, all locks it had acquired are released, and the remaining transaction or transactions are then allowed to proceed.) Information about such a series of events cannot be captured by the snapshot monitor because, in all likelihood, the deadlock cycle will have been broken long before a snapshot can be taken. An event monitor, on the other hand, could be used to capture such information because it would be activated the moment the deadlock cycle was detected.

By default, whenever a DB2 9 database is created, a deadlock event monitor named DB2DETAILDEADLOCK is defined for that database; the DB2DETAILDEADLOCK event monitor starts automatically when a connection to the database is established, or whenever the database is activated. When this monitor is active, diagnostic information is collected on the first occurrence of a deadlock, allowing for investigation into the cause without requiring a reproduction.

If this monitor is deleted and no other deadlock event monitor exists, you can still troubleshoot locking issues using the SYSIBMADM.SNAPLOCK and SYSIBMADM.SNAPLOCKWAIT snapshot monitor administrative views (or the corresponding SNAP_GET_LOCK() and SNAP_GET_LOCKWAIT() snapshot monitor table functions).

Unlike the snapshot monitor, which resides in the background and is always available, event monitors are special objects that must be created. You create event monitors by executing the CREATE EVENT MONITOR SQL statement. The basic syntax for this statement is:

```
CREATE EVENT MONITOR [EventMonName]
FOR [DATABASE |
      BUFFERPOOLS |
      TABLESPACES |
      TABLES |
      DEADLOCKS <WITH DETAILS <HISTORY <VALUES>>> |
      CONNECTIONS <WHERE [EventCondition]> |
      STATEMENTS <WHERE [EventCondition]>  |
      TRANSACTIONS <WHERE [EventCondition]> , ...]
WRITE TO [PIPE [PipeName] |
          TABLE (TABLE [TableName]) <BLOCKED | NONBLOCKED>|
          FILE [DirectoryName] <BLOCKED | NONBLOCKED>]
[MANUALSTART | AUTOSTART]
```

where:

EventMonName   Identifies the name to be assigned to the event monitor that is to bc created.

EventCondition   Identifies a condition that is used to determine for which CONNECTION, STATEMENT, or TRANSACTION events monitor data is to be collected.

TableName   Identifies the name assigned to the database table to which all event monitor data collected is to be written.

PipeName   Identifies the name assigned to the named pipe to which all event monitor data collected is to be written.

DirectoryName   Identifies the name assigned to the directory to which one or more files containing event monitor data are to be written.

As you can see by examining the syntax of the CREATE EVENT MONITOR statement, when an event monitor is created, the type of event to be monitored must be specified; Table 5.3 lists the event types available, along with the type of information that is collected for each type and details on when the data is actually collected.

Table 5.3 Event Monitor Types		
Event Type	**Data Collected**	**When Data Is Collected**
DATABASE	The values of all database level counters.	When the database is deactivated or when the last application connected to the database disconnects.
BUFFERPOOLS	The values of all buffer pool counters, prefetchers, and page cleaners, as well as direct I/Os for each buffer pool used.	When the database is deactivated or when the last application connected to the database disconnects.
TABLESPACES	The values of all buffer pool counters, prefetchers, page cleaners, and direct I/Os for each table space used.	When the database is deactivated or when the last application connected to the database disconnects.
TABLES	The number of rows read and the number of rows written for each table.	When the database is deactivated or when the last application connected to the database disconnects.
DEADLOCKS	Comprehensive information regarding applications involved, including the identification of participating SQL statements (along with statement text) and a list of locks being held.	When a deadlock cycle is detected.
CONNECTIONS	The values of all application level counters.	When an application that is connected to the database disconnects.
STATEMENTS	Statement start/stop time, amount of CPU used, text of dynamic SQL statements, SQLCA (the return code of the SQL statement), and other metrics such as fetch count. For partitioned databases: amount of CPU used, execution time, table information, and table queue information.	When an SQL statement finishes executing. For partitioned databases: when a subsection of an SQL statement finishes executing.
TRANSACTIONS	Transaction start/stop time, previous transaction time, and amount of CPU consumed, along with locking and logging metrics. (Transaction records are not generated if database is using two-phase commit processing and an X/Open XA Interface.)	When a transaction is terminated (by a COMMIT or a ROLLBACK statement).
Adapted from Table 9 on pages 60–61 of the *DB2 System Monitor Guide and Reference* manual.		

The location to which all monitor data collected is to be written must be specified as well; output from an event monitor can be written to one or more database tables, one or more external files, or a named pipe. Table event monitors and pipe event monitors stream event records directly to the table or named pipe specified. File event monitors, on the other hand, stream event records to a series of eight-character numbered files that have the extension ".evt" (for example, 00000000.evt, 00000001.evt, 00000002.evt, etc.).

Thus, if you wanted to create an event monitor that captures the values of all application-level counters and writes them to a database table named CONN_DATA every time an application that is connected to a database terminates its connection, you could do so by executing a CREATE EVENT MONITOR statement that looks something like this:

```
CREATE EVENT MONITOR conn_events
FOR CONNECTIONS
WRITE TO TABLE TABLE(conn_data)
```

On the other hand, if you wanted to create an event monitor that captures historical information about SQL statements that have been executed within the current transaction when a deadlock cycle occurs and writes all data collected to a directory named /export/home/DL_DATA, you could do so by executing a CREATE EVENT MONITOR statement that looks something like this:

```
CREATE EVENT MONITOR dl_events
FOR DEADLOCKS WITH DETAILS HISTORY
WRITE TO FILE '/export/home/DL_DATA'
```

Activating event monitors

Like the snapshot monitor, event monitors will begin collecting monitor data as soon as the database with which they are associated is activated or a connection to the database is established—provided the AUTOSTART option was specified when the event monitor was created. If the MANUALSTART option was used instead, or if neither option was specified (in which case the MANUALSTART option is used by default), an event monitor must be activated before it will begin collecting data. Event monitors are activated (and deactivated) by executing the SET EVENT MONITOR SQL statement.

When an event monitor is activated (started), it sits quietly in the background and waits for one of the events it is associated with to occur. Immediately after an event being monitored takes place, the event monitor collects monitor data associated with the event that triggered it and writes all data collected to the event monitor's target location. Thus, the event itself controls when monitor data is collected—unlike with the snapshot monitor, no special steps are required to capture the monitor data.

Other Troubleshooting Tools

Along with the database system monitor, several others utilities are available to help a database administrator isolate and identify problems with a system, database, or application. Some of the more popular troubleshooting utilities include the Bind File Description tool, the DB2 memory tracker utility, and the DB2 Problem Determination tool. In this section, we'll take a closer look at each.

The DB2 Bind File Description Tool

The DB2 Bind File Description Tool can be used to examine and to verify the SQL statements within a bind file, as well as to display the precompile options used to create the bind file. The DB2 Bind File Description Tool is invoked by executing the db2bfd command. The syntax for this command is:

```
db2bfd <-b> <-s> <-v> <-h> [BindFileName]
```

where:

BindFileName   Identifies, by name, the bind file whose contents are to be retrieved and displayed.

All options shown with this command are described in Table 5.4.

Table 5.4 db2bfd Command Options	
Option	**Meaning**
-b	Specifies that the bind file header is to be displayed.
-s	Specifies that the SQL statements in the bind file are to be displayed.
-v	Specifies that host variable declarations in the bind file are to be displayed.
-h	Displays help information. When this option is specified, all other options are ignored, and only the help information is displayed.

Thus, if you wanted to see the contents of a bind file named DB29TEST.BND, you could do so by executing a db2bfd command that looks something like this:

```
db2bfd -b -s -v db29test.bnd
```

The DB2 Memory Tracker

The DB2 memory tracker utility is used to produce a complete report of memory status for instances, databases, and agents. This utility provides the following information about memory pool allocation:

- Current size

- Maximum size (hard limit)

- Largest size (high water mark)

- Type (identifier indicating function for which memory will be used)

- Agent who allocated pool (only if the pool is private)

(This information is also available from the snapshot monitor.)

The DB2 memory tracker is invoked by executing the db2mtrk command. The syntax for this command is:

```
db2mtrk
<-i>
<-d>
<-p
<-m | -w>
<-r [Interval] <Count>>
<-v>
<-h>
```

where:

Interval   Identifies the number of seconds to wait between subsequent calls to the DB2 memory tracker.

Count   Identifies the number of times to repeat calls to the DB2 memory tracker.

All other options shown with this command are described in Table 5.5.

Table 5.5 db2mtrk Command Options	
Option	Meaning
-i	Specifies that information about instance level memory is to be collected and displayed.
-d	Specifies that information about database level memory is to be collected and displayed.
-p	Specifies that information about private memory is to be collected and displayed
-m	Specifies that maximum values for each memory pool is to be collected and displayed.
-w	Specifies that high watermark values for each memory pool is to be collected and displayed.
-v	Indicates that verbose output is to be returned.
-h	Displays help information. When this option is specified, all other options are ignored, and only the help information is displayed.

Thus, if you wanted to see how memory is utilized by the active databases on a system, you could do so by executing a db2mtrk command that looks something like this:

```
db2mtrk -d
```

The DB2 Problem Determination Tool

The DB2 Problem Determination tool is used to obtain quick and immediate information from the DB2 database system memory sets, without acquiring any latches. Two benefits to collecting information without latching include faster data retrieval and no competition for engine resources. However, because the DB2 Problem Determination tool works directly with memory, it is possible to retrieve information that is changing as it is being collected; hence, the data retrieved might not be completely accurate. (A signal handler is used to prevent the DB2 Problem Determination tool from aborting abnormally when changing memory pointers are encountered. However, this can result in messages such as "Changing data structure forced command termination" to appear in the output produced.) Nonetheless, this tool can be extremely helpful for problem determination.

If you want to capture information about the database management system when a specific SQLCODE, ZRC code or ECF code occurs, this can be accomplished using the db2pdcfg -catch command. (The db2pdcfg command can be used to set flags in the DB2 database memory sets to influence database system behavior.) When the errors are caught, the DB2 callout script (db2cos) is launched. This script can be dynamically altered to run any db2pd command, operating system command, or any other command needed to identify and solve a problem.

The DB2 Problem Determination tool is invoked by executing the `db2pd` command. The basic syntax for this command is:

```
db2pd
<- version | -v >
<-inst>
<[-database | -db] [DatabaseName] ,...>
<-alldatabases | -alldbs>
<-full>
<-everything>
<-hadr [-db [DatabaseName] | -alldbs]>
<-utilities>
<-applications [-db [DatabaseName] | -alldbs]>
<-agents>
<-transactions [-db [DatabaseName] | -alldbs]>
<-bufferpools [-db [DatabaseName] | -alldbs]>
<-logs [-db [DatabaseName] | -alldbs]>
<-locks [-db [DatabaseName] | -alldbs]>
<-tablespaces [-db [DatabaseName] | -alldbs]>
<-dynamic [-db [DatabaseName] | -alldbs]>
<-static [-db [DatabaseName] | -alldbs]>
<-fcm>
<-memsets>
<-mempools>
<-memblocks>
<-dbmcfg>
<-dbcfg [-db [DatabaseName] | -alldbs]>
<-catalogcache [-db [DatabaseName] | -alldbs]>
<-tcbstats [-db [DatabaseName] | -alldbs]>
<-reorg [-db [DatabaseName] | -alldbs]>
<-recovery [-db [DatabaseName] | -alldbs]>
<-reopt [-db [DatabaseName] | -alldbs]>
<-osinfo>
<-storagepaths [-db [DatabaseName] | -alldbs]>
<-pages [-db [DatabaseName] | -alldbs]>
<-stack [all | [ProcessID]]>
<-repeat [Interval] <[Count]>>
<-command [CmdFileName]>
<-file [OutFileName]>
<-interactive>
<-h | -help>
```

where:

DatabaseName   Identifies, by name, the database with which the DB2 Problem Determination tool is to interact.

ProcessID	Identifies the process, by ID, for which a stack trace file is to be produced.
Interval	Identifies the number of seconds to wait between subsequent calls to the DB2 Problem Determination tool.
Count	Identifies the number of time to repeat calls to the DB2 Problem Determination tool.
CmdFileName	Identifies the name assigned to an ASCII format file that contains DB2 Problem Determination tool command options that are to be used.
OutFile	Identifies the name of the file to which information returned by the DB2 Problem Determination tool is to be written.

All other options shown with this command are described in Table 5.6.

Table 5.6 db2pd Command Options	
Option	**Meaning**
-version | -v	Specifies that the current version and service level of the installed DB2 product is to be collected and displayed.
-inst	Specifies that all instance level information available is to be collected and displayed.
-alldatabases | -alldbs	Specifies that the utility is to attach to all memory sets of all available databases.
-full	Specifies that all output is to be expanded to its maximum length. (If this option is not specified, output is truncated to save space on the display.)
-everything	Specifies that all options are to be used and that information is to be collected and displayed for all databases on all database partition servers that are local to the server.
-hadr	Specifies that information about high availability disaster recovery (HADR) is to be collected and displayed.
-utilities	Specifies that information about utilities is to be collected and displayed.
-applications	Specifies that information about applications is to be collected and displayed.
-agents	Specifies that information about agents is to be collected and displayed.
-transactions	Specifies that information about active transactions is to be collected and displayed.

Table 5.6 db2pd Command Options (continued)	
Option	Meaning
-bufferpools	Specifies that information about buffer pools is to be collected and displayed.
-logs	Specifies that information about transaction log files is to be collected and displayed.
-locks	Specifies that information about locks is to be collected and displayed.
-tablespaces	Specifies that information about table spaces is to be collected and displayed.
-dynamic	Specifies that information about the execution of dynamic SQL statements is to be collected and displayed.
-static	Specifies that information about the execution of static SQL and packages is to be collected and displayed.
-fcm	Specifies that information about the fast communication manager is to be collected and displayed.
-memsets	Specifies that information about memory sets is to be collected and displayed.
-mempools	Specifies that information about memory pools is to be collected and displayed.
-memblocks	Specifies that information about memory blocks is to be collected and displayed.
-dbmcfg	Specifies that information about current DB2 Database Manager configuration parameter settings is to be collected and displayed.
-dbcfg	Specifies that information about current database configuration parameter settings is to be collected and displayed.
-catalogcache	Specifies that information about the catalog cache is to be collected and displayed.
-tcbstats	Specifies that information about tables and indexes is to be collected and displayed.
-reorg	Specifies that information about table and data partition reorganization is to be collected and displayed.
-recovery	Specifies that information about recovery activity is to be collected and displayed.
-reopt	Specifies that information about cached SQL statements that were reoptimized using the REOPT ONCE option is to be collected and displayed.
-osinfo	Specifies that operating system information is to be collected and displayed.
-storagepaths	Specifies that information about the automatic storage paths defined for the database is to be collected and displayed.
-pages	Specifies that information about buffer pool pages is to be collected and displayed.

Table 5.6 db2pd Command Options (continued)	
Option	Meaning
-stack	Specifies that stack trace information is to be collected and displayed.
-repeat	Specifies that the command is to be repeated after the specified number of seconds for the specified number of times.
-command	Specifies that db2pd commands that are stored in the specified in the file are to be executed.
-file	Specifies that all information collected is to be written to the specified file.
-interactive	Indicates that values specified for the DB2PDOPT environment variable are to be overridden when running the db2pd command.
-help | -h	Displays help information. When this option is specified, all other options are ignored, and only the help information is displayed.

So if you wanted to determine how many transactions are to be processed during the roll-forward phase of a recovery operation for a database named SAMPLE, you could do so by executing a db2pd command that looks something like this:

```
db2pd -recovery -db sample
```

On the other hand, if you wanted to monitor the progress of a RUNSTATS operation, you could do so by executing a db2pd command that looks something like this:

```
db2pd -utilities
```

There is no minimum connection requirement for executing the db2pd command. However, if a database-level option is specified, that database must be active before the requested information can be returned.

Practice Questions

Question 1

Which of the following queries can be used to obtain information about how buffer pools defined for a database named SAMPLE are being utilized?

○ A. SELECT * FROM SNAPSHOT_INFO ('sample', BUFFERPOOL)

○ B. SELECT * FROM SNAPSHOT_BP ('sample', −1)

○ C. SELECT * FROM TABLE(SNAPSHOT_INFO('sample', BUFFERPOOL)) AS snap_info

○ D. SELECT * FROM TABLE(SNAP_GET_BP('sample', -1)) AS snap_info

Question 2

Which of the following snapshot administrative views contains information that can be used to determine how many pages are being read from disk and how many pages are being read from memory?

○ A. SYSIBMADM.BP_HITRATIO

○ B. SYSIBMADM.BP_READ_IO

○ C. SYSIBMADM.BP_WRITE_IO

○ D. SYSIBMADM.APPL_PERFORMANCE

Question 3

Which of the following statements is NOT true about the SNAP_WRITE_FILE() stored procedure?

○ A. Snapshot data collected by the SNAP_WRITE_FILE() procedure can be viewed by issuing queries containing snapshot table functions.

○ B. The SNAP_WRITE_FILE() procedure is used to provide users who do not have SYSADM, SYSCTRL, SYSMAINT, or SYSMON authority the ability to access snapshot monitor data.

○ C. The SNAP_WRITE_FILE() procedure is used to capture snapshot monitor data and save the information collected to files, which can then be read with any text editor.

○ D. Special request type values can be specified with the SNAP_WRITE_FILE() procedure to limit the scope of monitor data that is collected.

Question 4

Which of the following queries will NOT return snapshot information about locks that have been acquired in a database named SAMPLE?

○ A. SELECT LOCK_OBJECT_TYPE, LOCK_MODE FROM
     SYSIBMADM.SNAPLOCK

○ B. SELECT LOCK_OBJECT_TYPE, LOCK_MODE FROM
     TABLE(SNAP_GET_LOCK(NULL, –1)) AS t

○ C. SELECT LOCK_OBJECT_TYPE, LOCK_MODE FROM
     TABLE(SNAP_GET_LOCK('SAMPLE', –1)) AS t

○ D. SELECT LOCK_OBJECT_TYPE, LOCK_MODE FROM
     TABLE(SNAP_GET_LOCK(CAST(NULL AS VARCHAR(20)), –1)) AS t

Question 5

Which of the following is NOT a true statement about DEADLOCK event monitors?

○ A. By default, a DEADLOCK event monitor is automatically created when a
     DB2 9 database is created.

○ B. Once created, the default DEADLOCK event monitor cannot be deleted.

○ C. The default DEADLOCK event monitor is activated when a connection to
     the database is first established.

○ D. DEADLOCK event monitor data is collected at the time a deadlock cycle is
     detected.

Question 6

Which of the following statements will create an event monitor that captures the values of all application-level counters and writes them to a table named CONN_DATA every time a database connection is terminated?

○ A. CREATE EVENT MONITOR conn_events FOR CONNECTIONS WRITE TO
     TABLE TABLE(conn_data)

○ B. CREATE EVENT MONITOR conn_events FOR CONNECTIONS WITH
     DETAILS WRITE TO TABLE TABLE(conn_data)

○ C. CREATE EVENT MONITOR conn_events FOR CONNECTIONS WRITE
     HISTORY TO TABLE TABLE(conn_data)

○ D. CREATE EVENT MONITOR conn_events FOR CONNECTIONS CAPTURE
     DETAILS WRITE TO TABLE TABLE(conn_data)

Question 7

A database administrator dropped the DB2DETAILDEADLOCK event monitor shortly after creating a new DB2 9 database. Assuming no other event monitors exist, which two of the following operations can be performed to troubleshoot locking issues?

❑ A. Recreate the DB2DETAILEDDEADLOCK event monitor by executing the CREATE DEFAULT DEADLOCK MONITOR command.

❑ B. Create a query that references the SNAPSHOT_APPL and SNAPSHOT_APPLINFO snapshot monitor table functions.

❑ C. Create a new deadlock event monitor by executing the CREATE EVENT MONITOR command.

❑ D. Create a query that references the SNAPSHOT_LOCK and SNAPSHOT_LOCKWAIT snapshot monitor table functions.

❑ E. Query the SYSIBMADM.SNAPLOCK and SYSIBMADM.SNAPLOCKWAIT snapshot administrative views

Question 8

Which of the following statements is NOT true about the DB2 Problem Determination tool (db2pd)?

○ A. db2pd is used to obtain quick and immediate information from the DB2 database system memory sets.

○ B. db2pd does not require a connection to an active database in order to obtain information about it.

○ C. db2pd can be used to obtain information about an instance that has stopped prematurely.

○ D. Because db2pd works directly with memory, it is possible to retrieve information that will change as it is being collected.

Question 9

Which of the following best describes the functionality of db2mtrk?

○ A. It reports how memory is being managed by the Self Tuning Memory Manager.

○ B. It estimates the memory requirements for a database, based on values assigned to the memory-related Database Manager configuration parameters.

○ C. It produces report of memory status for instances, databases and agents.

○ D. It recommends memory-related Database Manager configuration parameter values that will improve memory utilization.

Question 10

Which of the following parameter can be used with db2pd to get information about the total number of transactions to be performed during the roll forward phase of a recovery operation?

- ○ A. -transactions
- ○ B. -recovery
- ○ C. -utilities
- ○ D. -logs

Answers

Question 1

The correct answer is **D**. With earlier versions of DB2, the only way to capture snapshot monitor data was by executing the GET SNAPSHOT command or by calling its corresponding API from an application program. With DB2 UDB version 8.1, the ability to capture snapshot monitor data by constructing a query that referenced one of 20 snapshot monitor table functions available was introduced. If you wanted to take a snapshot that contains data collected on buffer pools associated with the currently connected database using the DB2 V8.1 SNAPSHOT_BP() snapshot monitor table function, you could do so by executing the following query:

```
SELECT * FROM TABLE (SNAPSHOT_BP
       (CAST (NULL AS CHAR), -1) AS snap_info
```

Although these functions are still available and can be used in DB2 9, they have been depreciated. Now, snapshot monitor data can be obtained by querying special administrative views or by using a new set of SQL table functions. Each DB2 9 snapshot monitor table function returns the same information as the corresponding administrative view, but the function allows you to retrieve information for a specific database instead of the current connected database. The syntax used to construct a query that references a DB2 9 snapshot monitor table function is the same as that used to reference a DB2 8.1 function—only the function names have changed. Therefore, if you wanted to obtain snapshot monitor buffer pool information for a database named SAMPLE using the SNAP_GET_BP() table function you could do so by constructing a query that looks something like this:

```
SELECT * FROM TABLE(SNAP_GET_BP('sample', -1)) AS snap_info
```

Question 2

The correct answer is **A**. The SYSIBMADM.BP_HITRATIO snapshot administrative view returns buffer pool hit ratios, including total hit ratio, data hit ratio, XDA hit ratio and index hit ratio, for all buffer pools and all database partitions in the currently connected database. The ratio of physical reads to logical reads gives the hit ratio for the buffer pool. The lower the hit ratio, the more the data is being read from disk rather than the buffer pool, which can be a more costly operation.

The SYSIBMADM.BP_READ_IO snapshot administrative view returns buffer pool read performance information; the SYSIBMADM.BP_WRITE_IO snapshot administrative view returns buffer pool write performance information; and the SYSIBMADM. APPL_PERFORMANCE snapshot administrative view returns information about the rate of rows selected versus rows read per application.

Question 3

The correct answer is **C**. The SNAP_WRITE_FILE() procedure can be used to capture snapshots of monitor data and save the information collected to files on the database server. Once the snapshot data has been saved to a file, any user—including users who do not have SYSADM, SYSCTRL, SYSMAINT, or SYSMON authority—can issue queries with the corresponding snapshot table functions, specifying (NULL, NULL) as input values for database-level table functions, and (NULL) for database manager level table functions. The monitor data they receive is pulled from the files generated by the SNAP_WRITE_FILE () stored procedure.

Question 4

The correct answer is **B**. Snapshot information about locks that have been acquired in a database named SAMPLE can be obtained by querying the SYSIBMADM.SNAPLOCK administrative table or by constructing a query that references the SNAP_GET_LOCK() table function. Such a query looks something like this:

```
SELECT * FROM TABLE (SNAP_GET_LOCK('[DBName]', [PartitionNum]) AS
[CorrelationName]
```

where:

DBName   Identifies the database for which snapshot monitor data is to be collected.

PartitionNum   Identifies the database partition for which snapshot monitor data is to be collected.

CorrelationName   Identifies the name that is to be assigned to the result data set produced by the query.

If you want to capture snapshot monitor data for the current partition in a partitioned database environment, you can do so by specifying the value -1 for the *PartitionNum* parameter; if you want to capture snapshot monitor data for the current connected database, you could do so by specifying a null value for the *DBName* parameter, either by using empty single quotation marks (' ') or by using a cast operation to produce a null character value— for example, CAST (NULL AS CHAR).

Question 5

The correct answer is **B**. If you are familiar with the concept of deadlocks, you may recall that a special process known as the deadlock detector runs quietly in the background and "wakes up" at predefined intervals to scan the locking system in search of a deadlock cycle. If a deadlock cycle exists, the deadlock detector randomly selects one of the transactions involved in the cycle to roll back and terminate. (The transaction that is rolled back and terminated receives an SQL error code, all locks it had acquired are released, and the remaining transaction(s) are then allowed to proceed.) Information about such a series of events can be captured, the moment the deadlock cycle is detected.

By default, whenever a DB2 9 database is created, a deadlock event monitor is defined for that database and this event monitor is activated when a connection to the database is first established, or whenever the database is activated.

Question 6

The correct answer is **A**. You create event monitors by executing the CREATE EVENT MONITOR SQL statement; the basic syntax for this statement is:

```
CREATE EVENT MONITOR [EventMonName]
FOR [DATABASE |
     BUFFERPOOLS |
     TABLESPACES |
     TABLES |
     DEADLOCKS <WITH DETAILS <HISTORY <VALUES>>> |
     CONNECTIONS <WHERE [EventCondition]> |
     STATEMENTS <WHERE [EventCondition]>  |
     TRANSACTIONS <WHERE [EventCondition]> , ...]
WRITE TO [PIPE [PipeName] |
          TABLE (TABLE [TableName]) <BLOCKED | NONBLOCKED>|
          FILE [DirectoryName] <BLOCKED | NONBLOCKED>]
[MANUALSTART | AUTOSTART]
```

where:

EventMonName   Identifies the name to be assigned to the event monitor that is to be created.

EventCondition   Identifies a condition that is used to determine for which CONNECTION, STATEMENT, or TRANSACTION events monitor data is to be collected.

TableName   Identifies the name assigned to the database table to which all event monitor data collected is to be written.

PipeName   Identifies the name assigned to the named pipe to which all event monitor data collected is to be written.

DirectoryName Identifies the name assigned to the directory to which one or more files containing event monitor data are to be written.

Thus, if you wanted to create an event monitor that captures the values of all application-level counters and writes them to a database table named CONN_DATA every time an application that is connected to a database terminates its connection, you could do so by executing a CREATE EVENT MONITOR statement that looks something like this:

```
CREATE EVENT MONITOR conn_events
FOR CONNECTIONS
WRITE TO TABLE TABLE(conn_data)
```

Question 7

The correct answers are **C** and **E**. By default, whenever a DB2 9 database is created, a deadlock event monitor named DB2DETAILDEADLOCK is defined for that database; the DB2DETAILDEADLOCK event monitor starts automatically when a connection to the database is established, or whenever the database is activated. When this monitor is active, diagnostic information is collected on the first occurrence of a deadlock, allowing for investigation into the cause without requiring a reproduction.

If this monitor is deleted and no other deadlock event monitor exists, you can still troubleshoot locking issues using the SYSIBMADM.SNAPLOCK and SYSIBMADM.SNAPLOCKWAIT snapshot monitor administrative views (or the corresponding SNAP_GET_LOCK() and SNAP_GET_LOCKWAIT() snapshot monitor table functions). You can also create a new deadlock event monitor by executing a command that looks something like this:

```
CREATE EVENT MONITOR dl_events
FOR DEADLOCKS WITH DETAILS HISTORY
WRITE TO FILE '/export/home/DL_DATA'
```

Question 8

The correct answer is **C**. The DB2 Problem Determination tool (db2pd) is used to obtain quick and immediate information from the DB2 database system memory sets, without acquiring any latches. Two benefits to collecting information without latching include faster data retrieval and no competition for engine resources. However, because the DB2 Problem Determination tool works directly with memory, it is possible to retrieve information that is changing as it is being collected; hence the data retrieved might not be completely accurate. (A signal handler is used to prevent the DB2 Problem Determination tool from aborting abnormally when changing memory pointers are encountered. However, this can result in messages such as "Changing data structure forced command termination" to appear in the output produced.) Nonetheless, this tool can be extremely helpful for problem determination.

There is no minimum connection requirement for executing the db2pd command; if a database-level option is specified, that database must be active before the requested information can be returned. The db2pd command cannot be used to obtain information about a stopped instance.

Question 9

The correct answer is **C**. The DB2 memory tracker utility is used to produce a complete report of memory status for instances, databases and agents. This utility provides the following information about memory pool allocation:

- Current size

- Maximum size (hard limit)

- Largest size (high water mark)

- Type (identifier indicating function for which memory will be used)

- Agent who allocated pool (only if the pool is private)

(This information is also available from the Snapshot monitor.)

The DB2 memory tracker is invoked by executing the db2mtrk command.

Question 10

The correct answer is **B**. The –recovery option of the db2pd command is used to specify that information about recovery activity is to be collected and displayed. If you take a close look at the on-line help for this option, you will discover that when this option is used, the following information is returned:

Option	Meaning
Recovery Status	The internal recovery status.
Current Log	The current log being used by the recovery operation.
Current LSN	The current log sequence number.
Job Type	The type of recovery being performed. The possible values are: ● Crash recovery. ● Roll-forward recovery on either the database or a table space.
Job ID	The job identifier.
Job Start Time	The time the recovery operation started.
Job Description	A description of the recovery activity. The possible values are: ● Table space Roll-forward Recovery ● Database Roll-forward Recovery ● Crash Recovery
Invoker Type	How the recovery operation was invoked. The possible values are: ● User ● DB2
Total Phases	The number of phases required to complete the recovery operation.
Current phase	The current phase of the recovery operation.
Phase	The number of the current phase in the recovery operation.
Forward phase	The first phase of roll-forward recovery. This phase is also known as the REDO phase.
Backward phase	The second phase of roll-forward recovery. This phase is also known as the UNDO phase.
Metric	The units of work. The possible values are: ● Bytes. ● Extents. ● Rows. ● Pages. ● 5. Indexes
TotWkUnits	The total number of units of work (UOW) to be done for this phase of the recovery operation.
TotCompUnits	The total number of UOWs that have been completed.

The –utilities option is used to specify that information about utilities is to be collected and displayed; the –transactions option is used to specify that information about active transactions is to be collected and displayed; and the –log option is used to specify that information about transaction log files is to be collected and displayed.

CHAPTER 6

High Availability

Ten and one-half percent (10.5%) of the DB2 9 for Linux, UNIX, and Windows Database Administration Upgrade exam (Exam 736) is designed to evaluate your knowledge of transactions and transaction logging and to test your ability to back up and restore a database and to successfully establish a high availability disaster recovery (HADR) environment. The questions that make up this portion of the exam are intended to evaluate the following:

- Your ability to use the RECOVER DATABASE command

- Your knowledge of high availability disaster recovery (HADR)

This chapter is designed to introduce you to the backup and recovery tools that are available with DB2 and to show you how to both restore a damaged database with the RECOVER DATABASE command and how to set up an HADR environment.

Transactions and Transaction Logging

A transaction (also known as a unit of work) is a sequence of one or more SQL operations grouped together as a single unit, usually within an application process. The initiation and termination of a single transaction defines points of data consistency within a database; either the effects of all operations performed within a transaction are applied to the database and made permanent (committed), or the effects of all operations performed are backed out (rolled back), and the database is returned to the state it was in before the transaction was initiated.

In most cases, transactions are initiated the first time an executable SQL statement is executed after a connection to a database has been made or immediately after a preexisting transaction has been terminated. Once initiated, transactions can be implicitly terminated using a feature known as "automatic commit" (in which case, each executable SQL statement is treated as a single transaction, and any changes made by that statement are applied to the database if the statement executes successfully or are discarded if the statement fails), or they can be explicitly terminated by executing the COMMIT or the ROLLBACK SQL statement. The basic syntax for these two statements is:

```
COMMIT <WORK>
```

and

```
ROLLBACK <WORK>
```

When the COMMIT statement is used to terminate a transaction, all changes made to the database since the transaction began are made permanent. On the other hand, when the ROLLBACK statement is used, all changes made are backed out, and the database is returned to the state it was in just before the transaction began.

Transaction logging is simply a process used to keep track of changes made to a database (by a transaction), *as they occur*. Each time an update or a delete operation is performed, the page containing the record to be updated/deleted is retrieved from storage and copied to the appropriate buffer pool, where it is then modified by the update/delete operation. (If a new record is created by an insert operation, that record is created directly in the appropriate buffer pool.) Once the record has been modified (or inserted), a record reflecting the modification/insertion is written to the log buffer, which is simply another designated storage area in memory. If an insert operation is performed, a record containing the new row is written to the log buffer; if a delete operation is performed, a record containing the row's original values is written to the log buffer; and if an update operation is performed, a record containing the row's original values, combined with the row's new values, is written to the log buffer. (If replication has not been enabled, an Exclusive OR operation is performed using the "before" and "after" rows and the results are written to the log buffer.)

Whenever buffer pool I/O page cleaners are activated, the log buffer becomes full, or a transaction is terminated (by being committed or rolled back), all records stored in the log buffer are immediately written to one or more log files stored on disk. As soon as all log records associated with a particular transaction have been externalized to one or more log files, the effects of the transaction itself are recorded in the database (i.e., executed against the appropriate table space containers for permanent storage). The modified data pages remain in memory, where they can be quickly accessed if necessary—eventually, they will be overwritten as newer pages are retrieved from storage. The transaction logging process can be seen in Figure 6–1.

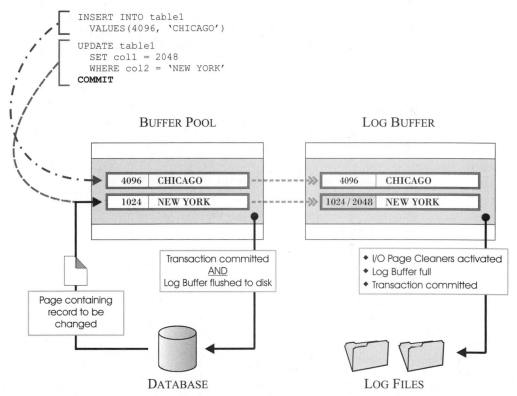

Figure 6–1: The transaction logging process.

Since log records are externalized frequently and because changes made by a particular transaction are only externalized to the database when the transaction itself is successfully terminated, the ability to return a database to a consistent state after a failure occurs is guaranteed—when the database is restarted, log records are analyzed, and each record that has a corresponding COMMIT record is reapplied to the database; every record that does not have a corresponding COMMIT record is either ignored or backed out (which is why "before" and "after" information is recorded for all update operations).

Database Recovery Concepts

Over time, a database can encounter any number of problems, including power interruptions, storage media failure, and application abends. All of these can result in database failure, and each failure scenario requires a different recovery action.

The concept of backing up a database is the same as that of backing up any other set of data files: you make a copy of the data and store it on a different medium where it can be accessed in the event the original becomes damaged or destroyed. The simplest way to back up a database is to shut it down to ensure that no further transactions are processed and then back it up using the Backup utility provided with DB2. Once a backup image has been created, you can use it to rebuild the database later if for some reason it becomes damaged or corrupted.

The process of rebuilding a database is known as recovery, and three types of recovery are available with DB2:

- Crash recovery

- Version recovery

- Roll-forward recovery

Crash Recovery

Crash recovery is performed by using information stored in the transaction log files to complete any committed transactions that were in memory (but had not yet been externalized to storage) when the transaction failure occurred, roll back any incomplete transactions found, and purge any uncommitted transactions from memory. Once a database is returned to a consistent and usable state, it has attained what is known as a "point of consistency." Crash recovery is illustrated in Figure 6–2.

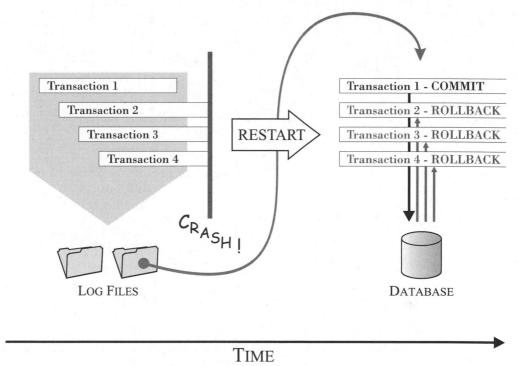

Figure 6–2: Crash recovery.

A crash recovery operation is initiated by executing the RESTART DATABASE command.

Version Recovery

Version recovery is the process used to return a database to the state it was in at the time a particular backup image was made. Version recovery is performed by replacing the current version of a database with a previous version, using a copy that was made with a backup operation—the entire database is rebuilt using a backup image that was created earlier. Unfortunately, when a version recovery is performed, all changes made to the database since the backup image used was created are lost. Version recovery is illustrated in Figure 6–3.

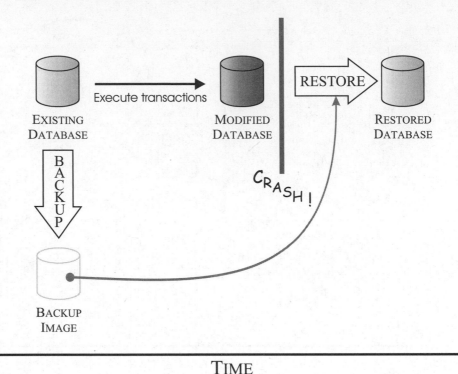

Execute transactions

EXISTING
DATABASE

MODIFIED
DATABASE

RESTORE

RESTORED
DATABASE

B
A
C
K
U
P

CRASH!

BACKUP
IMAGE

TIME

Figure 6–3: Version recovery.

A version recovery operation is initiated by executing the RESTORE DATABASE command; database backup images needed for version recovery operations are generated by executing the BACKUP DATABASE command.

Roll-Forward Recovery

Roll-forward recovery takes version recovery one step farther by rebuilding a database or one or more individual table spaces using a backup image and replaying information stored in transaction log files to return the database/table spaces to the state they were in at an exact point in time. In order to perform a roll-forward recovery operation, you must have archival logging enabled, you must have either a full backup image of the database or a complete set of table space backup images available, and you must have access to all archived log files that have been created since the backup image(s) were made. Roll-forward recovery is illustrated in Figure 6–4.

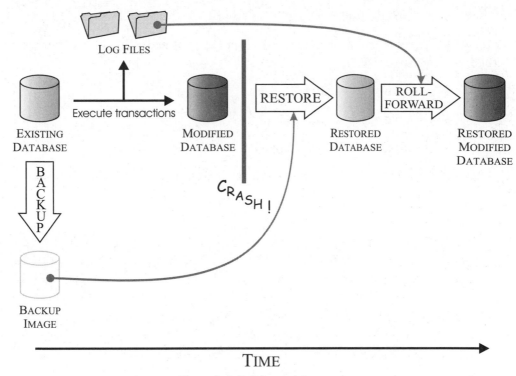

Figure 6–4: Roll-forward recovery.

A roll-forward recovery operation is initiated by executing the ROLLFORWARD DATABASE command.

A Word About the Recovery History File

When a new DB2 database is created, a special file known as the recovery history file is built as part of the database creation process. This file is used to log historical information about specific actions that are performed against the database with which the file is associated. Specifically, records are written to the recovery history file whenever any of the following actions are performed:

- A backup image of any type is created.

- A version recovery operation is performed either on the database or on one of its table spaces.

- A table is loaded, using the Load utility.

- A roll-forward recovery operation is performed either on the database or on one of its table spaces.

- A table space is altered.

- A table space is quiesced.

- Data in a table is reorganized, using the REORG utility.

- Statistics for a table are updated, using the RUNSTATS utility.

- A table is deleted (dropped).

In addition to identifying the event that was performed, each entry in the recovery history file identifies the date and time the event took place, how the event took place, and the table spaces and tables that were affected and, if the action was a backup operation, the location where the backup image produced was stored, along with information on how to access this image. And because the recovery history file contains image location information for each backup image available, it can act as a tracking and verification mechanism during version recovery operations.

The DB2 Recover Utility

While the RESTORE DATABASE command can be used to return a database to the state it was in at the time a backup image was made, and the ROLLFORWARD DATABASE command can be used to replay information recorded in a database's transaction log files to return a database to the state it was in at a specific point in time, if you have a current recovery history file, you can perform both operations in a single step using the Recover utility.

Introduced in DB2 9, the Recover utility performs the necessary restore and roll-forward operations to recover a database to a specific point in time, based on information found in the recovery history file. The Recovery utility is invoked by executing the RECOVER DATABASE command. The basic syntax for this command is:

```
RECOVER [DATABASE | DB] [DatabaseAlias]
<TO [PointInTime] <USING [UTC | LOCAL] TIME>>
<ON ALL DBPARTITIONNUMS>
<USER [UserName] <USING [Password]>>
```

```
<USING HISTORY FILE ([HistoryFile])>
<OVERFLOW LOG PATH ([LogDirectory] ,...)>
<RESTART>
```

or

```
RECOVER [DATABASE | DB] [DatabaseAlias]
<TO END OF LOGS
     <ON ALL DBPARTITIONNUMS |
      ON DBPARTITIONNUM<S> ([PartitionNum],...)>>
<USER [UserName] <USING [Password]>>
<USING HISTORY FILE ([HistoryFile])>
<OVERFLOW LOG PATH ([LogDirectory] ,...)>
<RESTART>
```

where:

DatabaseAlias   Identifies the alias assigned to the database associated with the backup image that is to be used to perform a version recovery operation.

PointInTime   Identifies a specific point in time, identified by a timestamp value in the form *yyyy-mm-dd-hh.mm.ss.nnnnnn* (year, month, day, hour, minutes, seconds, microseconds), to which the database is to be rolled forward. (Only transactions that took place before and up to the date and time specified will be reapplied to the database.)

PartitionNum   Identifies, by number, one or more database partitions (identified in the db2nodes.cfg file) that transactions are to be rolled forward on. In a partitioned database environment, the Recover utility must be invoked from the catalog partition of the database.

UserName   Identifies the name assigned to a specific user under whom the recovery operation is to be performed.

Password   Identifies the password that corresponds to the name of the user under whom the recovery operation is to be performed.

HistoryFile   Identifies the name assigned to the recovery history log file that is to be used by the Recovery utility.

LogDirectory   Identifies the directory that contains offline archived log files that are to be used to perform the roll-forward portion of the recovery operation.

Thus, if you wanted to perform a full recovery operation on a database named SAMPLE (which already exists) using information stored in the recovery history file, you could do so by executing a RECOVER DATABASE command that looks something like this:

```
RECOVER DATABASE sample
TO END OF LOGS
```

On the other hand, if you wanted to restore a database named SAMPLE and roll it forward to an extremely old point in time that is no longer contained in the current recovery history file, you could do so by executing a RECOVER DATABASE command that looks something like this (assuming you have a copy of an older recovery history file available):

```
RECOVER DATABASE sample
TO 2005-01-31-04.00.00
USING HISTORY FILE (/home/user/old2005files/db2rhist.asc)
```

It is important to note that if the Recover utility successfully restores a database, but for some reason fails while attempting to roll it forward, the Recover utility will attempt to continue the previous recover operation, without redoing the restore phase. If you want to force the Recover utility to redo the restore phase, you need to execute the RECOVER DATABASE command with the RESTART option specified. There is no way to explicitly restart a recovery operation from a point of failure.

High Availability Disaster Recovery (HADR)

High availability disaster recovery (HADR) is a DB2 database replication feature that provides a high availability solution for both partial and complete site failures. HADR protects against data loss by replicating data changes from a source database, called the primary, to a target database, called the standby. In an HADR environment, applications can only access the current primary database— synchronization with the standby database occurs by rolling forward transaction log data that is generated on the primary database and shipped to the standby database. And with HADR, you can choose the level of protection you want from potential loss of data by specifying one of three synchronization modes: synchronous, near synchronous, or asynchronous.

HADR is designed to minimize the impact to a database system when a partial or a complete site failure occurs. A partial site failure can be caused by a hardware, network, or software (DB2 or operating system) malfunction. Without HADR, a partial site failure requires restarting the server and the instance where one or more DB2 databases reside. The length of time it takes to restart the server and the instance is unpredictable; if the transaction load was heavy at the time of the partial site failure, it can take several minutes before a database is returned to a consistent state and made available for use. With HADR, the standby database can take over in seconds. Furthermore, you can redirect the clients that were using the original primary database to the standby database (which is now the new primary database) by using automatic client reroute or retry logic in the applications that interact with the database. After the failed original primary server is repaired, it can rejoin the HADR pair as a standby database if both copies of the database can be made consistent. And once the original primary database is reintegrated into the HADR pair as the standby database, you can switch the roles so that the original primary database once again functions as the primary database. (This is known as failback operation.)

A complete site failure can occur when a disaster, such as a fire, causes the entire site to be destroyed. Because HADR uses TCP/IP to communicate between a primary and a standby database, the databases can reside it two different locations. For example, your primary database might be located at your head office in one city, whereas your standby database is located at your sales office in another city. If a disaster occurs at the primary site, data availability is maintained by having the remote standby database take over as the primary database.

Requirements for HADR Environments

To achieve optimal performance with HADR, the system hosting the standby database should consist of the same hardware and software as the system where the primary database resides. If the system hosting the standby database has fewer resources than the system hosting the primary database, the standby database may not be able to keep up with the transaction load generated by the primary database.

This can cause the standby database to fall behind or the performance of the primary database to suffer. But more importantly, if a failover situation occurs, the new primary database may not have the resources needed to adequately service the client applications. And because buffer pool operations performed on the primary database are replayed on the standby database, it is important that the primary and standby database servers have the same amount of memory.

IBM recommends that you use identical host computers for the HADR primary and standby databases. (If possible, they should be manufactured by the same vendor and have the same architecture.) Furthermore, the operating system on the primary and standby database servers should be the same version, including patch level. You can violate this rule for a short time during a rolling upgrade, but use extreme caution when doing so. A TCP/IP interface must also be available between the HADR host machines, and a high-speed, high-capacity network should be used to connect the two.

The DB2 software installed on both the primary and the standby database server must have the same bit size (32 or 64), and the version of DB2 used for the primary and standby databases must be identical; for example, both must be either version 8 or version 9. During rolling upgrades, the modification level (for example, the fix pack level) of the database system for the standby database can be later than that of the primary database for a short while. However, you should not keep this configuration for an extended period of time. The primary and standby databases will not connect to each other if the modification level of the database system for the primary database is later than that of the standby database. Therefore, fix packs must always be applied to the standby database system first.

Both the primary and the standby database must be a single-partition database, and they both must have the same database name; however, they do not have to be stored on the same database path. The amount of storage space allocated for transaction log files should also be the same on both the primary and the standby database server; the use of raw devices for transaction logging is not supported. (Archival logging is performed only by the current primary database.)

Table space properties such as table space name, table space type (DMS, SMS, or Automatic Storage), table space page size, table space size, container path, container size, and container type (raw device, file, or directory) must be identical on the primary and standby databases. When you issue a table space statement such as

CREATE TABLESPACE, ALTER TABLESPACE, or DROP TABLESPACE on the primary database, it is replayed on the standby database. Therefore, you must ensure that the table space containers involved with such statements exist on both systems before you issue the table space statement on the primary database. (If you create a table space on the primary database, and log replay fails on the standby database because the containers are not available, the primary database does not receive an error message stating that the log replay failed.) Automatic storage databases are fully supported, including replication of ALTER DATABASE statements. Similar to table space containers, the storage paths specified must exist on both the primary and the standby server.

Once an HADR environment has been established, the following restrictions apply:

- Reads on the standby database are not supported; clients cannot connect to the standby database.

- Self Tuning Memory Manager (STMM) can be run only on the current primary database.

- Backup operations cannot be performed on the standby database.

- Redirected restore is not supported. That is, HADR does not support redirecting table space containers. However, database directory and log directory changes are supported.

- Load operations with the COPY NO option specified are not supported.

Setting Up an HADR Environment

The process of setting up an HADR environment is fairly straightforward. After ensuring that the systems to be used as primary and secondary server are identical and that a TCP/IP connection exists between them, you simply perform the following tasks, in the order shown:

1. Determine the host name, host IP address, and the service name or port number for both the primary and the secondary database server.

   If a server has multiple network interfaces, ensure that the HADR host name or IP address maps to the intended interface. You will need to allocate separate HADR ports for each protected database—these cannot be the same as the ports that have been allocated to the instance. The host name can map to only one IP address.

2. Create the standby database by restoring a backup image or initializing a split mirror copy of the database that is to serve as the primary database.

It is recommended that you do not issue the ROLLFORWARD DATABASE command on the standby database after the restore operation or split mirror initialization. The results of performing a roll-forward recovery operation might differ slightly from replaying the logs on the standby database using HADR. If the primary and standby databases are not identical when HADR is started, an error will occur.

When setting up the standby database using the RESTORE DATABASE command, it is recommended that the REPLACE HISTORY FILE option be used; use of the following options should be avoided: TABLESPACE, INTO, REDIRECT, and WITHOUT ROLLING FORWARD.

3. Set the HADR configuration parameters on both the primary and the standby databases.

After the standby database has been created, but before HADR is started, the HADR configuration parameters shown in Table 7.2 need to be set.

Table 7.2 HADR-Specific Database Configuration Parameters		
Parameter	Value Range / Default	Description
hadr_db_role	N/A	Read-only. Indicates the current role of the database, if it is part of a high availability disaster recovery (HADR) environment. Valid values are STANDARD, PRIMARY, or STANDBY.
hadr_local_host	Any valid character string Default: NULL	Specifies the local host for high availability disaster recovery (HADR) TCP communication. Either a host name or an IP address can be used.
hadr_local_svc	Any valid character string Default: NULL	Specifies the TCP service name or port number for which the local high availability disaster recovery (HADR) process accepts connections.
hadr_remote_host	Any valid character string Default: NULL	Specifies the TCP/IP host name or IP address of the remote high availability disaster recovery (HADR) node.
hadr_remote_inst	Any valid character string Default: NULL	Specifies the instance name of the remote server. Administration tools, such as the Control Center, use this parameter to contact the remote server. High availability disaster recovery (HADR) also checks whether a remote database requesting a connection belongs to the declared remote instance.
hadr_remote_svc	Any valid character string Default: NULL	Specifies the TCP service name or port number that will be used by the remote high availability disaster recovery (HADR) node.
hadr_syncmode	SYNC, NEARSYNC, ASYNC Default: NEARSYNC	Specifies the synchronization mode to use for high availability disaster recovery (HADR). This determines how primary log writes are synchronized with the standby database when the systems are in peer state. Valid values for this configuration parameter are SYNC (this mode provides the greatest protection against transaction loss, but at a higher cost of transaction response time), NEARSYNC (this mode provides somewhat less protection against transaction loss, in exchange for a shorter transaction response time than that of SYNC mode), and ASYNC (this mode has the highest probability of transaction loss in the event of primary failure, in exchange for the shortest transaction response time among the three modes).
hadr_timeout	1–4,294,967,295 Default: 120	Specifies the time (in seconds) that the high availability disaster recovery (HADR) process waits before considering a communication attempt to have failed.

4. Connect to the standby instance and start HADR on the standby database.

   HADR is started by executing the START HADR command. The basic syntax for this command is:

   ```
   START HADR ON [DATABASE | DB] [DatabaseAlias]
   <USER [UserName] <USING [Password]>>
   AS [PRIMARY <BY FORCE> | SECONDARY]
   ```

   where:

DatabaseAlias	Identifies the alias assigned to the database for which HADR is to be started.
UserName	Identifies the name assigned to a specific user under whom HADR is to be started.
Password	Identifies the password that corresponds to the name of the user under whom HADR is to be started.

   Thus, if you wanted to start HADR on a database named SAMPLE and indicate that it is to act as a standby database, you could do so by executing a START HADR command that looks something like this:

   ```
   START HADR ON DATABASE sample AS STANDBY
   ```

5. Connect to the primary instance and start HADR on the primary database.In this case, you would execute a START HADR command that looks something like this:

   ```
   START HADR ON DATABASE sample AS PRIMARY
   ```

   You can also set up an HADR environment using the Set Up HADR Databases Wizard, which can be activated by selecting the High Availability Disaster Recovery action from the Databases menu found in the Control Center. Figure 6–5 shows how the first page of the Set Up HADR Databases Wizard might look immediately after it is activated.

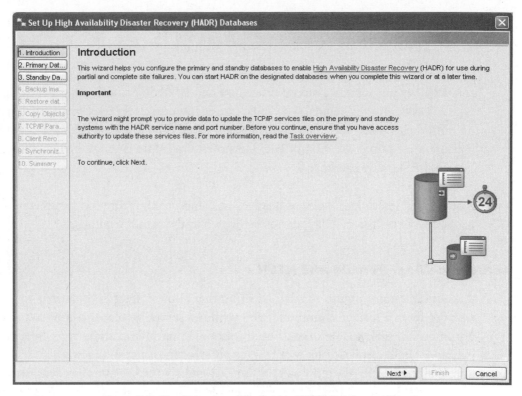

Figure 6–5: The first page of the Set Up HADR Databases Wizard.

Once an HADR environment has been established, the following operations will be replicated automatically in the standby database whenever they are performed on the primary database:

- Execution of Data Definition Language (DDL) statements (CREATE, ALTER, DROP)

- Execution of Data Manipulation Language (DML) statements (INSERT, UPDATE, DELETE)

- Buffer pool operations

- Table space operations (as well as storage-related operations performed on automatic storage databases)

- Online reorganization

- Offline reorganization

- Changes to metadata for stored procedures and user-defined functions (UDFs)

HADR does not replicate stored procedure and UDF object and library files. If this type of replication is needed, you must physically create the files on identical paths on both the primary and standby databases. (If the standby database cannot find the referenced object or library file, the stored procedure or UDF invocation will fail on the standby database.)

Non-logged operations, such as changes to database configuration parameters and to the recovery history file, are not replicated to the standby database.

Automatic Client Reroute and HADR

Automatic client reroute is a DB2 feature that allows client applications to recover from a loss of communication with the server so that the application can continue its work with minimal interruption. (If automatic client reroute is not enabled, client applications will receive an error message indicating that a connect attempt has failed due to a timeout and no further attempts will be made to establish a connection with the server.) However, rerouting is possible only when an alternate database location has been specified at the server and the TCP/IP protocol is used.

The automatic client reroute feature can be used with HADR to make client applications connect to the new primary database immediately after a takeover operation. In fact, if you set up HADR using the Set Up High Availability Disaster Recovery (HADR) Databases Wizard, automatic client reroute is enabled by default. If you set up HADR manually, you can enable the automatic client reroute feature by executing the UPDATE ALTERNATE SERVER FOR DATABASE command; automatic client reroute does not use the values stored in the *hadr_remote_host* and *hadr_remote_svc* database configuration parameters.

For example, suppose you have cataloged a database named SALES on a client workstation as being located at host named SVR1. Database SALES is the primary database in an HADR environment and its corresponding standby database, also named SALES, resides on host named SVR2 and listens on port number 456. To enable automatic client reroute, you simply specify an alternate server for the SALES database stored on host SVR1 by executing the following command:

```
UPDATE ALTERNATE SERVER FOR DATABASE sales
USING HOSTNAME svr2 PORT 456
```

Once this command is executed, the client must connect to host SVR1 to obtain the alternate server information. Then, if a communication error occurs between the client and the SALES database at host SVR1, the client will first attempt to reconnect to the SALES database on host SVR1. If this fails, the client will then attempt to establish a connection with the standby SALES database located on host SVR2.

Practice Questions

Question 1

Which of the following is NOT a valid statement about the RECOVER DATABASE command?

○ A. The RECOVER DATABASE command performs the necessary restore and roll-forward operations to recover a database.

○ B. The RECOVER DATABASE command only rolls a database forward to the end of logs; it cannot roll forward to a specific point in time.

○ C. The RECOVER DATABASE command can only be used successfully if the recovery history file for the database is available.

○ D. The RECOVER DATABASE command cannot continue a previously unsuccessful recover operation from the point of failure; if a failure occurs, the recovery operation must be performed again.

Question 2

Which of the following statements is NOT true regarding the use of the RECOVER DATABASE command in a partitioned database environment?

○ A. If the recovery operation is to a specific point in time, it affects all partitions found in the db2nodes.cfg file.

○ B. If the recovery operation is to the end of logs, it only affects the partitions that are specified with the RECOVER DATABASE command.

○ C. The RECOVER DATABASE command can be invoked from any database partition provided it is prefixed with db2_all.

○ D. The RECOVER DATABASE command can only be used successfully if the recovery history file for the database is available.

Question 3

Given two servers named SVR1 and SVR2 with a database named SALES on SRV1, in what order should the following steps be performed to set up an HADR environment using SRV2 as a standby server?

    a) Backup the SALES database on SVR1.

    b) Determine the host name, host IP address, and the service name or port number for SVR1 and SVR2.

    c) Start HADR on SVR2.

    d) Set the HADR configuration parameters on SVR1 and SVR2.

    e) Restore the SALES database on SVR2.

    f) Start HADR on SVR1.

○ A. b, a, e, d, f, c

○ B. b, d, f, c, a, e

○ C. b, a, e, d, c, f

○ D. f, c, b, d, a, e

Question 4

Which of the following is NOT an operation that is replicated in an HADR environment?

○ A. Database configuration changes

○ B. Execution of Data Definition Language (DDL) statements

○ C. Online table reorganizations

○ D. Execution of Data Manipulation Language (DML) statements

Question 5

Which of the following is NOT supported in an HADR environment?

○ A. Automatic client reroute

○ B. Automatic storage databases

○ C. Write operations to the standby database

○ D. Single partitioned databases

Question 6

Which of the following is NOT a requirement for an HADR environment?

○ A. The operating system on the primary server and the standby server must be the same (including fix pack level).

○ B. The database path on the primary server and the standby server must be the same.

○ C. The DB2 software version and bit size (32 or 64) used on the primary server and the standby server must be the same.

○ D. Table spaces and table space containers on the primary server and the standby server must be identical.

Answers

Question 1

The correct answer is **B**. The Recover utility performs the necessary restore and roll-forward operations to recover a database to a specific point in time, based on information found in the recovery history file. (The Recovery utility is invoked by executing the RECOVER DATABASE command.) If the Recover utility successfully restores a database, but for some reason fails while attempting to roll it forward, the entire recovery operation must be performed again. There is no way to restart a recovery operation from a point of failure.

Question 2

The correct answer is **C**. In a partitioned database environment, the Recover utility must be invoked from the catalog partition of the database.

Question 3

The correct answer is **C**. After ensuring the systems to be used as primary and secondary server are identical and that a TCP/IP connection exists between them, you can establish an HADR environment by performing the following tasks, in the order shown:

1. Determine the host name, host IP address, and the service name or port number for both the primary and the secondary database server.

2. Create the standby database by restoring a backup image or initializing a split mirror copy of the database that is to serve as the primary database.

3. Set the HADR configuration parameters on both the primary and the standby databases.

4. Connect to the standby instance and start HADR on the standby database.

5. Connect to the primary instance and start HADR on the primary database.

Question 4

The correct answer is **A**. Once an HADR environment has been established, the following operations will be replicated automatically in the standby database whenever they are performed on the primary database:

- Execution of Data Definition Language (DDL) statements (CREATE, ALTER, DROP)

- Execution of Data Manipulation Language (DML) statements (INSERT, UPDATE, DELETE)

- Buffer pool operations

- Table space operations

- Online reorganization

- Offline reorganization

- Changes to metadata for stored procedures and user-defined functions (UDFs)

HADR does not replicate stored procedure and UDF object and library files. If this type of replication is needed, you must physically create the files on identical paths on both the primary and standby databases. (If the standby database cannot find the referenced object or library file, the stored procedure or UDF invocation will fail on the standby database.)

Non-logged operations, such as changes to database configuration parameters and to the recovery history file, are not replicated to the standby database.

Question 5

The correct answer is **C**. In an HADR environment, applications can only access the current primary database—synchronization with the standby database occurs by rolling forward transaction log data that is generated on the primary database and shipped to the standby database.

Question 6

The correct answer is **B**. Both the primary and the standby database must be a single-partition database and they both must have the same database name; however, they do not have to be stored on the same database path.

Security

T en and one-half percent (10.5%) of the DB2 9 for Linux, UNIX, and Windows Database Administration Upgrade exam (Exam 736) is designed to test your knowledge about the new mechanisms provided with DB2 9 to protect data and database objects against unauthorized access and modification. The questions that make up this portion of the exam are intended to evaluate the following:

- Your ability to identify the authentication types that are available with DB2 9

- Your knowledge of the mechanisms and steps needed to implement label-based access control (LBAC)

This chapter is designed to introduce you to the new authentication types that are available with DB2 9 and to show you how to implement LBAC to control access to columns and rows in a table or view.

Controlling Database Access

Every database management system must be able to protect data against unauthorized access and modification. DB2 uses a combination of external security services and internal access control mechanisms to perform this vital task. In most cases, three different levels of security are employed: The first level controls access to the instance under which a database was created, the second controls access to the database itself, and the third controls access to the data and data objects that reside within the database.

Authentication

The first security portal most users must pass through on their way to gaining access to a DB2 instance or database is a process known as *authentication*. The purpose of authentication is to verify that users really are who they say they are. Normally, authentication is performed by an external security facility that is not part of DB2. This security facility may be part of the operating system (as is the case with AIX, Solaris, Linux, HP-UX, Windows 2000/NT, and many others), may be a separate add-on product (for example, Distributed Computing Environment [DCE] Security Services), or may not exist at all (which is the case with Windows 95, Windows 98, and Windows Millennium Edition). If a security facility does exist, it must be presented with two specific items before a user can be authenticated: a unique user ID and a corresponding password. The user ID identifies the user to the security facility, and the password, which is information known only by the user and the security facility, is used to verify that the user is indeed who he or she claims to be.

Where Does Authentication Take Place?

Because DB2 can reside in environments composed of multiple clients, gateways, and servers, each of which may be running on a different operating system, deciding where authentication is to take place can be a daunting task. To simplify things, DB2 uses a parameter in each DB2 Database Manager configuration file (the *authentication* parameter) to determine how and where users are authenticated. Such a file is associated with every instance, and the value assigned to this parameter, often referred to as the *authentication type*, is set initially when an instance is created. Only one authentication type exists for each instance, and it controls access to that instance, as well as to all databases that fall under that instance's control.

The following authentication types are available:

> **SERVER.** Authentication occurs at the server workstation, using the security facility provided by the server's operating system. (The user ID and password provided by the user wishing to attach to an instance or connect to a database are compared to the user ID and password combinations stored at the server to determine whether the user is permitted to access the instance or database.) By default, this is the authentication type used when an instance is first created.

SERVER_ENCRYPT. Authentication occurs at the server workstation, using the security facility that is provided by the server's operating system. However, the password provided by the user wishing to attach to an instance or connect to a database stored on the server may be encrypted at the client workstation before it is sent to the server workstation for validation.

CLIENT. Authentication occurs at the client workstation or database partition where a client application is invoked, using the security facility that is provided by the client's operating system, assuming one is available. If no security facility is available, authentication is handled in a slightly different manner. The user ID and password provided by the user wishing to attach to an instance or connect to a database are compared to the user ID and password combinations stored at the client or node to determine whether the user is permitted to access the instance or the database.

KERBEROS. Authentication occurs at the server workstation, using a security facility that supports the Kerberos security protocol. This protocol performs authentication as a third-party service by using conventional cryptography to create a shared secret key. The key becomes the credentials used to verify the identity of the user whenever local or network services are requested; this eliminates the need to pass a user ID and password across the network as ASCII text. It should be noted that the KERBEROS authentication type is supported only on clients and servers that are using the Windows operating system. In addition, both client and server workstations must either belong to the same Windows domain or belong to trusted domains.

KRB_SERVER_ENCRYPT. Authentication occurs at the server workstation, using either the KERBEROS or the SERVER_ENCRYPT authentication method. If the client's authentication type is set to KERBEROS, authentication is performed at the server using the Kerberos security system. On the other hand, if the client's authentication type is set to anything other than KERBEROS, or if the Kerberos authentication service is unavailable, the server acts as if the SERVER_ENCRYPT authentication type was specified, and the rules of this authentication method apply.

Along with these traditional authentication types, four new authentication types are available with DB2 9. They are:

DATA_ENCRYPT. Authentication occurs at the server workstation, using the SERVER_ENCRYPT authentication method. In addition, the following data is encrypted before it is passed from client to server and from server to client:

- SQL and XQuery statements.

- SQL program variable data.

- Output data from the server processing of an SQL statement or XQuery expression, including a description of the data.

- Some or all of the result set data produced in response to a query.

- Large object (LOB) data streaming.

- SQLDA descriptors.

DATA_ENCRYPT_CMP. Authentication occurs at the server workstation, using the SERVER_ENCRYPT authentication method; all user data is encrypted before it is passed from client to server and from server to client. In addition, this authentication type provides compatibility for down-level products that do not support the DATA_ENCRYPT authentication type. Such products connect using the SERVER_ENCRYPT authentication type, and user data is not encrypted.

GSSPLUGIN. Authentication occurs at the server workstation, using a Generic Security Service Application Program Interface (GSS-API) plug-in. If the client's authentication type is not specified, the server returns a list of server-supported plug-ins (found in the *srvcon_gssplugin_list* database manager configuration parameter) to the client. The client then selects the first plug-in found in the client plug-in directory from the list. If the client does not support any plug-in in the list, the client is authenticated using the KERBEROS authentication method.

GSS_SERVER_ENCRYPT. Authentication occurs at the server workstation, using either the GSSPLUGIN or the SERVER_ENCRYPT authentication method. That is, if client authentication occurs through a GSS-API plug-in, the client is authenticated using the first client-supported plug-in found in the list of server-supported plug-ins. If the client does not support any of the plug-ins found in the server-supported plug-in list, the client is authenticated using the

KERBEROS authentication method. If the client does not support the Kerberos security protocol, the client is authenticated using the SERVER_ENCRYPT authentication method.

Authorities and Privileges

Once a user has been authenticated, and an attachment to an instance or a connection to a database has been established, the DB2 Database Manger evaluates any authorities and privileges that have been assigned to the user to determine what operations the user is allowed to perform. Privileges convey the rights to perform certain actions against specific database resources (such as tables and views). Authorities convey a set of privileges or the right to perform high-level administrative and maintenance/utility operations on an instance or a database. Authorities and privileges can be assigned directly to a user, or they can be obtained indirectly from the authorities and privileges that have been assigned to a group of which the user is a member. Together, authorities and privileges act to control access to the DB2 Database Manager for an instance, to one or more databases running under that instance's control, and to a particular database's objects. Users can work only with those objects for which they have been given the appropriate authorization—that is, the required authority or privilege. Figure 7–1 provides a hierarchical view of the authorities and privileges that are recognized by DB2 9.

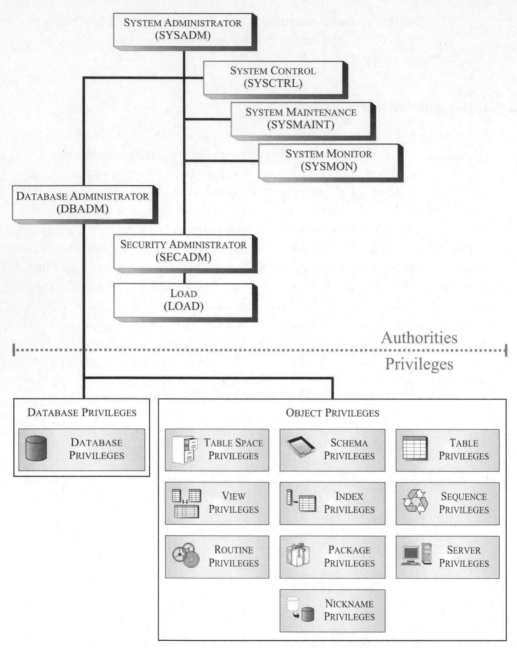

Figure 7–1: Hierarchy of the authorities and privileges available with DB2 9.

Securing Data with Label-Based Access Control (LBAC)

Label-based access control (LBAC) is a new security feature that uses one or more security labels to control who has read access and who has write access to individual rows and/or columns in a table or view. The United States and many other governments use LBAC models in which hierarchical classification labels such as CONFIDENTIAL, SECRET, and TOP SECRET are assigned to data based on its sensitivity. Access to data labeled at a certain level (for example, SECRET) is restricted to those users who have been granted that level of access or higher. With LBAC, you can construct security labels to represent any criteria your company uses to determine who can read or modify particular data values.

Security Administrator authority

One problem with the traditional security methods DB2 uses is that Security Administrators and Database Administrators have access to sensitive data stored in the databases they oversee. To solve this problem, LBAC-security administration tasks are isolated from all other tasks—only users with Security Administrator (SECADM) authority are allowed to configure LBAC elements.

Security Administrator (SECADM) authority is a special database level of authority that is designed to allow special users to configure various label-based access control (LBAC) elements to restrict access to one or more tables. Users who are granted this authority are allowed to perform only the following tasks:

- Create and drop security policies

- Create and drop security labels

- Grant and revoke security labels to and from individual users (using the GRANT SECURITY LABEL and REVOKE SECURITY LABEL SQL statements)

- Grant and revoke LBAC rule exemptions

- Grant and revoke SETSESSIONUSER privileges (using the GRANT SETSESSIONUSER SQL statement)

- Transfer ownership of any object not owned by the Security Administrator (by executing the TRANSFER OWNERSHIP SQL statement)

No other authority, including System Administrator authority, provides a user with these abilities.

Implementing Row-Level LBAC

Before you implement a row-level LBAC solution, you need to have a thorough understanding of the security requirement needs. Suppose you have a database that contains company sales data, and you want to control how senior executives, regional managers, and sales representatives access data stored in a table named SALES. Security requirements might dictate that access to this data should comply with these rules:

- Senior executives are allowed to view, but not update, all records in the table.

- Regional managers are allowed to view and update only records that were entered by sales representatives who report to them.

- Sales representatives are allowed to view and update only records of the sales they made.

Once the security requirements are known, you must then define the appropriate security policies and labels, create an LBAC-protected table (or alter an existing table to add LBAC protection), and grant the proper security labels to the appropriate users.

Defining a security label component

Security label components represent criteria that may be used to decide whether a user should have access to specific data. Three types of security label components can exist:

- A *set* is a collection of elements (character string values) where the order in which each element appears is not important.

- An *array* is an ordered set that can represent a simple hierarchy. In an array, the order in which the elements appear is important—the first element ranks higher than the second, the second ranks higher than the third, and so on.

- A *tree* represents a more complex hierarchy that can have multiple nodes and branches.

To create security label components, you execute one of the following CREATE SECURITY LABEL COMPONENT SQL statements:

```
CREATE SECURITY LABEL COMPONENT [ComponentName]
SET {StringConstant,...}
```

or

```
CREATE SECURITY LABEL COMPONENT [ComponentName]
ARRAY [StringConstant,...]
```

or

```
CREATE SECURITY LABEL COMPONENT [ComponentName]
TREE (StringConstant ROOT < StringConstant UNDER StringConstant >)]
```

where:

ComponentName   Identifies the name that is to be assigned to the security label component being created.

StringConstant   Identifies one or more string constant values that make up the valid array, set, or tree of values to be used by the security label component being created.

Thus, to create a security label component named SEC_COMP that contains a set of values whose order is insignificant, you would execute a CREATE SECURITY LABEL COMPONENT statement that looks something like this:

```
CREATE SECURITY LABEL COMPONENT sec_comp
SET {'CONFIDENTIAL', 'SECRET', 'TOP_SECRET'}
```

To create a security label component that contains an array of values listed from highest to lowest order, you would execute a CREATE SECURITY LABEL COMPONENT statement that looks something like this:

```
CREATE SECURITY LABEL COMPONENT sec_comp
ARRAY ['MASTER_CRAFTSMAN', 'JOURNEYMAN', 'APPRENTICE']
```

And to create a security label component that contains a tree of values that describe a company's organizational chart, you would execute a CREATE SECURITY LABEL COMPONENT statement that looks something like this:

```
CREATE SECURITY LABEL COMPONENT sec_comp
TREE ('EXEC_STAFF' ROOT,
             'N_MGR' UNDER 'EXEC_STAFF',
             'E_MGR' UNDER 'EXEC_STAFF',
             'S_MGR' UNDER 'EXEC_STAFF',
             'W_MGR' UNDER 'EXEC_STAFF',
             'C_MGR' UNDER 'EXEC_STAFF',
             'SALES_REP1' UNDER 'N_MGR',
             'SALES_REP2' UNDER 'W_MGR')
```

Defining a security policy

Security policies determine exactly how a table is to be protected by LBAC. Specifically, a security policy identifies the following:

- What security label components will be used in the security labels that will be part of the policy

- What rules will be used when security label components are compared (at this time, only one set of rules is supported: DB2LBACRULES)

- Which optional behaviors will be used when accessing data protected by the policy

Every LBAC-protected table must have one (and only one) security policy associated with it. Rows and columns in that table can be protected only with security labels that are part of that security policy; all protected data access must adhere to the rules of that policy. You can have multiple security policies within a single database, but you can't have more than one security policy protecting any given table.

To create a security policy, execute the CREATE SECURITY POLICY SQL statement as follows:

```
CREATE SECURITY POLICY [PolicyName]
COMPONENTS [ComponentName ,...]
WITH DB2LBACRULES
<[OVERRIDE | RESTRICT] NOT AUTHORIZED
    WRITE SECURITY LABEL>
```

where:

PolicyName   Identifies the name that is to be assigned to the security policy being created.

ComponentName Identifies, by name, one or more security label components that are to be part of the security policy being created.

The [OVERRIDE | RESTRICT] NOT AUTHORIZED WRITE SECURITY LABEL option specifies the action to be taken when a user who is not authorized to write the security label explicitly specified with INSERT and UPDATE statements attempts to write data to the protected table. By default, the value of a user's security label, rather than an explicitly specified security label, is used for write access during insert and update operations (OVERRIDE NOT AUTHORIZED WRITE SECURITY LABEL). If the RESTRICT NOT AUTHORIZED WRITE SECURITY LABEL option is used, insert and update operations will fail if the user isn't authorized to write the explicitly specified security label to the protected table.

Therefore, to create a security policy named SEC POLICY that is based on the SEC_COMP security label component created earlier, you would execute a CREATE SECURITY POLICY statement that looks something like this:

```
CREATE SECURITY POLICY sec_policy
COMPONENTS sec_comp
WITH DB2LBACRULES
```

Defining security labels

Security labels describe a set of security criteria and are used to protect data against unauthorized access or modification. Security labels are granted to users who are allowed to access or modify protected data; when users attempt to access or modify protected data, their security label is compared to the security label protecting the data to determine whether the access or modification is allowed. Every security label is part of exactly one security policy, and a security label must exist for each security label component found in the security policy.

Security labels are created by executing the CREATE SECURITY LABEL SQL statement. The syntax for this statement is:

```
CREATE SECURITY LABEL [LabelName]
[COMPONENT [ComponentName] [StringConstant] ,...]
```

where:

LabelName   Identifies the name that is to be assigned to the security label being created. The name specified must be qualified with a security policy name and must not match an existing security label for the security policy specified.

ComponentName   Identifies, by name, a security label component that is part of the security policy specified as the qualifier for the *LabelName* parameter.

StringConstant   Identifies one or more string constant values that are valid elements of the security label component specified in the *ComponentName* parameter.

Thus, to create a set of security labels for the security policy named SEC_POLICY that was created earlier, you would execute a set of CREATE SECURITY LABEL statements that look something like this:

```
CREATE SECURITY LABEL sec_policy.exec_staff
COMPONENT sec_comp 'EXEC_STAFF'

CREATE SECURITY LABEL sec_policy.n_mgr
COMPONENT sec_comp 'N_MGR'

CREATE SECURITY LABEL sec_policy.e_mgr
COMPONENT sec_comp 'E_MGR'

CREATE SECURITY LABEL sec_policy.s_mgr
COMPONENT sec_comp 'S_MGR'

CREATE SECURITY LABEL sec_policy.w_mgr
COMPONENT sec_comp 'W_MGR'

CREATE SECURITY LABEL sec_policy.c_mgr
COMPONENT sec_comp 'C_MGR'

CREATE SECURITY LABEL sec_policy.sales_rep1
COMPONENT sec_comp 'SALES_REP1'

CREATE SECURITY LABEL sec_policy.sales_rep2
COMPONENT sec_comp 'SALES_REP2'
```

Creating a LBAC-protected table

Once you have defined the security policy and labels needed to enforce your security requirements, you're ready to create a table and configure it for LBAC protection. To configure a new table for row-level LBAC protection, you include a column with the data type DB2SECURITYLABEL in the table's definition and associate a security policy with the table using the SECURITY POLICY clause of the CREATE TABLE SQL statement.

So to create a table named SALES and configure it for row-level LBAC protection using the security policy named SEC_POLICY created earlier, you would execute a CREATE TABLE statement that looks something like this instead:

```
CREATE TABLE corp.sales (
      sales_rec_id    INTEGER NOT NULL,
      sales_date      DATE WITH DEFAULT,
      sales_rep       INTEGER,
      region          VARCHAR(15),
      manager         INTEGER,
      sales_amt       DECIMAL(12,2),
      margin          DECIMAL(12,2),
      sec_label       DB2SECURITYLABEL)
   SECURITY POLICY sec_policy
```

To configure an existing table named SALES for row-level LBAC protection using a security policy named SEC_POLICY, you would execute an ALTER TABLE statement that looks like this instead:

```
ALTER TABLE corp.sales
   ADD COLUMN sec_label DB2SECURITYLABEL
   ADD SECURITY POLICY sec_policy
```

However, before you can execute such an ALTER TABLE statement, you must be granted a security label for write access that is part of the security policy that will be used to protect the table (which, in this case is SEC_POLICY). Otherwise, you won't be able to create the DB2SECURITYLABEL column.

Granting security labels to users

Once the security policy and labels needed to enforce your security requirements have been defined, and a table has been enabled for LBAC-protection, you must grant the proper security labels to the appropriate users and indicate whether they are to have read access, write access, or full access to data that is protected by that label. Security labels are granted to users by executing a special form of the GRANT SQL statement. The syntax for this form of the GRANT statement is:

```
GRANT SECURITY LABEL [LabelName]
TO USER [UserName]
[FOR ALL ACCESS | FOR READ ACCESS | FOR WRITE ACCESS]
```

where:

LabelName Identifies the name of an existing security label. The name specified must be qualified with the security policy name that was used when the security label was created.

UserName Identifies the name of the user to which the security label is to be granted.

Thus, to give a user named USER1 the ability to read data protected by the security label SEC_POLICY.EXEC_STAFF, you would execute a GRANT statement that looks like this:

```
GRANT SECURITY LABEL sec_policy.exec_staff
TO USER user1 FOR READ ACCESS
```

Putting row-level LBAC into action

To enforce the security requirements listed earlier, we must first give users the ability to perform DML operations against the SALES table by executing the following GRANT statements, as a user with SYSADM or DBADM authority:

```
GRANT ALL PRIVILEGES ON TABLE corp.sales TO exec_staff;
GRANT ALL PRIVILEGES ON TABLE corp.sales TO n_manager;
GRANT ALL PRIVILEGES ON TABLE corp.sales TO e_manager;
GRANT ALL PRIVILEGES ON TABLE corp.sales TO s_manager;
GRANT ALL PRIVILEGES ON TABLE corp.sales TO w_manager;
GRANT ALL PRIVILEGES ON TABLE corp.sales TO c_manager;
GRANT ALL PRIVILEGES ON TABLE corp.sales TO sales_rep1;
GRANT ALL PRIVILEGES ON TABLE corp.sales TO sales_rep2;
```

Next, we must grant the proper security labels to the appropriate users and indicate whether they are to have read access, write access, or full access to data that is protected by that label. This is done by executing the following GRANT statements, this time as a user with SECADM authority:

```
GRANT SECURITY LABEL sec_policy.exec_staff
TO USER exec_staff FOR READ ACCESS;

GRANT SECURITY LABEL sec_policy.n_mgr
TO USER n_manager FOR ALL ACCESS;

GRANT SECURITY LABEL sec_policy.e_mgr
TO USER e_manager FOR ALL ACCESS;

GRANT SECURITY LABEL sec_policy.s_mgr
TO USER s_manager FOR ALL ACCESS;

GRANT SECURITY LABEL sec_policy.w_mgr
TO USER w_manager FOR ALL ACCESS;

GRANT SECURITY LABEL sec_policy.c_mgr
TO USER c_manager FOR ALL ACCESS;

GRANT SECURITY LABEL sec_policy.sales_rep1
TO USER sales_rep1 FOR ALL ACCESS;

GRANT SECURITY LABEL sec_policy.sales_rep2
TO USER sales_rep2 FOR ALL ACCESS;
```

Now, suppose user SALES_REP1 adds three rows to the SALES table by executing the following SQL statements:

```
INSERT INTO corp.sales VALUES (1, DEFAULT, 1, 'NORTH', 5,
    1000.50, 500.00,
    SECLABEL_BY_NAME('SEC_POLICY', 'SALES_REP1'));

INSERT INTO corp.sales VALUES (2, DEFAULT, 1, 'NORTH', 5,
    2000.00, 400.00,
    SECLABEL_BY_NAME('SEC_POLICY', 'SALES_REP1'));

INSERT INTO corp.sales VALUES (3, DEFAULT, 1, 'NORTH', 5,
    4500.90, 850.00,
    SECLABEL_BY_NAME('SEC_POLICY', 'SALES_REP1'));
```

SALES_REP1 has been given read/write access to the table using the SEC_POLICY.SALES_REP1 security label, so the statements execute successfully. Next, user SALES_REP2 adds two additional rows to the SALES table by executing the following SQL statements:

```
INSERT INTO corp.sales VALUES (4, DEFAULT, 1, 'WEST', 20,
     1000.50, 500.00,
     SECLABEL_BY_NAME('SEC_POLICY', 'SALES_REP2'));

INSERT INTO corp.sales VALUES (5, DEFAULT, 1, 'WEST', 20,
     3200.00, 600.00,
     SECLABEL_BY_NAME('SEC_POLICY', 'SALES_REP2'));
```

Because SALES_REP2 has also been given read/write access to the table using the SEC_POLICY.SALES_REP2 security label, the rows are successfully inserted.

Now, when user EXEC_STAFF queries the SALES table, all five records entered will appear (because the security label SEC_POLICY.EXEC_STAFF is the highest level in the security policy's security label component tree). However, if user EXEC_STAFF attempts to insert additional records or update an existing record, an error will be generated because user EXEC_STAFF is allowed only to read the data (only read access was granted).

When user N_MANAGER queries the table, only records entered by the user SALES_REP1 will be displayed; the user W_MANAGER will see only records entered by the user SALES_REP2; and the users E_MANAGER, S_MANAGER, and C_MANAGER will not see any records at all. (SALES_REP1 reports to N_MANAGER, SALES_REP2 reports to W_MANAGER; no other managers have a sales representative reporting to them.)

And finally, when SALES_REP1 or SALES_REP2 queries the SALES table, they will see only the records they personally entered. Likewise, they can update only the records they entered.

If you want to retrieve values stored in a DB2SECURITYLABEL column and display them in a human-readable format, you can do so by using the SECLABEL_TO_CHAR() scalar function in a SELECT statement – provided you have the LBAC credentials needed to see the row. Thus, if user EXEC_STAFF executes the following query:

```
SELECT sales_rec_id, sec_label,
   SECLABEL_TO_CHAR('SEC_POLICY', sec_label) AS s_l2
FROM corp. sales
```

The following results will be returned:

SALES_REC_ID	SEC_LABEL	S_L2
1	x'0000000000000001	SALES_REP1
2	x'0000000000000001	SALES_REP1
3	x'0000000000000001	SALES_REP1
4	x'0000000000000010	SALES_REP2
5	x'0000000000000010	SALES_REP2

Implementing Column-Level LBAC

To illustrate how column-level LBAC is employed, let's assume you want to control how Human Resources (HR) staff members, managers, and employees are going to access data stored in a table named EMPLOYEES. For this scenario, the security requirements are as follows:

- Name, gender, department, and phone number information can be viewed by all employees.

- Hire date, salary, and bonus information (in addition to name, gender, department, and phone number information) can be seen only by managers and HR staff members.

- Employee ID and Social Security Number information can be seen only by HR staff members. Additionally, HR staff members are the only users who can create and modify employee records.

Once again, after the security requirements have been identified, the next steps are to define the appropriate security component, policies, and labels; create the table that will house the data; alter the table to add LBAC protection; and grant the proper security labels to the appropriate users.

Defining security label components, security policies, and security labels

Because an array of values, listed from highest to lowest order, would be the best way to implement the security requirements just outlined, you could create the security component needed by executing a CREATE SECURITY LABEL COMPONENT statement (as a user with SECADM authority) that looks something like this:

```
CREATE SECURITY LABEL COMPONENT sec_comp
ARRAY ['CONFIDENTIAL', 'CLASSIFIED', 'UNCLASSIFIED']
```

After the appropriate security label component has been created, you can create a security policy named SEC_POLICY that is based on the SEC_COMP security label component by executing a CREATE SECURITY POLICY statement (as a user with SECADM authority) that looks like this:

```
CREATE SECURITY POLICY sec_policy
COMPONENTS sec_comp
WITH DB2LBACRULES
```

Earlier, we saw that security labels are granted to users who are allowed to access or modify LBAC-protected data; when users attempt to access or modify protected data, their security label is compared to the security label protecting the data to determine whether the access or modification is allowed. But before security labels can be granted, they must first be defined. To create a set of security labels for the security policy named SEC_POLICY that was just created, you would execute the following set of CREATE SECURITY LABEL statements (as a user with SECADM authority):

```
CREATE SECURITY LABEL sec_policy.confidential
COMPONENT sec_comp 'CONFIDENTIAL'

CREATE SECURITY LABEL sec_policy.classified
COMPONENT sec_comp 'CLASSIFIED'

CREATE SECURITY LABEL sec_policy.unclassified
COMPONENT sec_comp 'UNCLASSIFIED'
```

Keep in mind that every security label is part of exactly one security policy, and a security label must exist for each security label component found in that security policy.

Creating a LBAC-protected table and granting privileges and security labels to users

Earlier, we saw that in order to configure a new table for row-level LBAC protection, you must associate a security policy with the table being created with the SECURITY POLICY clause of the CREATE TABLE SQL statement. The same is true if column-level LBAC protection is desired. Therefore, to create a table named EMPLOYEES and associate it with a security policy named SEC_POLICY, you would need to execute a CREATE TABLE statement that looks something like this:

```
CREATE TABLE hr.employees (
    emp_id      INTEGER NOT NULL,
    f_name      VARCHAR(20),
    l_name      VARCHAR(20),
    gender      CHAR(1),
    hire_date   DATE WITH DEFAULT,
    dept_id     CHAR(5),
    phone       CHAR(14),
    ssn         CHAR(12),
    salary      DECIMAL(12,2),
    bonus       DECIMAL(12,2))
  SECURITY POLICY sec_policy
```

Then, in order to enforce the security requirements identified earlier, you must give users the ability to perform the appropriate DML operations against the EMPLOYEES table. This is done by executing the following GRANT SQL statements (as a user with SYSADM or DBADM authority):

```
GRANT ALL PRIVILEGES ON TABLE hr.employees TO hr_staff;
GRANT SELECT ON TABLE hr.employees TO manager1;
GRANT SELECT ON TABLE hr.employees TO employee1;
```

Finally, you must grant the proper security label to the appropriate users and indicate whether they are to have read access, write access, or full access to data that is protected by that label. This is done by executing a set of GRANT statements (as a user with SECADM authority) that look something like this:

```
GRANT SECURITY LABEL sec_policy.confidential
TO USER hr_staff FOR ALL ACCESS;

GRANT SECURITY LABEL sec_policy.classified
TO USER manager1 FOR READ ACCESS;

GRANT SECURITY LABEL sec_policy.unclassified
TO USER employee1 FOR READ ACCESS;
```

Creating LBAC-protected columns

Once you've defined the security policy and labels needed to enforce your security requirements and have granted the appropriate privileges and security labels to users, you are ready to modify the table associated with the security policy and configure its columns for column-level LBAC protection. This is done by executing an ALTER TABLE statement that looks something like this:

```
ALTER TABLE hr.employees
      ALTER COLUMN emp_id SECURED WITH confidential
      ALTER COLUMN f_name SECURED WITH unclassified
      ALTER COLUMN l_name SECURED WITH unclassified
      ALTER COLUMN gender SECURED WITH unclassified
      ALTER COLUMN hire_date SECURED WITH classified
      ALTER COLUMN dept_id SECURED WITH unclassified
      ALTER COLUMN phone SECURED WITH unclassified
      ALTER COLUMN ssn SECURED WITH confidential
      ALTER COLUMN salary SECURED WITH classified
      ALTER COLUMN bonus SECURED WITH classified;
```

Here is where things get a little tricky. If you try to execute the ALTER TABLE statement shown as a user with SYSADM or SECADM authority, the operation will fail, and you will be presented with an error message that looks something like this:

```
SQL20419N For table "EMPLOYEES", authorization ID " " does not have LBAC
credentials that allow using the security label "CONFIDENTIAL" to protect
column "EMP_ID".  SQLSTATE=42522
```

That's because the only user who can secure a column with the "CONFIDENTIAL" security label is a user who has been granted *write access* to data that is protected by that label. In our scenario, this is the user HR_STAFF. So what happens when user HR_STAFF attempts to execute the preceding ALTER TABLE statement? Now a slightly different error message is produced:

```
SQL20419N For table "EMPLOYEES", authorization ID "HR_STAFF" does not
have LBAC credentials that allow using the security label "UNCLASSIFIED"
to protect column "F_NAME".  SQLSTATE=42522
```

Why? Because, by default, the LBAC rules set associated with the security policy assigned to the EMPLOYEES table allows the user HR_STAFF to write data only to columns or rows that are protected by the same security label that he/she has been granted.

DB2LBACRULES rules

An LBAC rule set is a predefined set of rules that is used when comparing security labels. Currently, only one LBAC rule set is supported (DB2LBACRULES), and as we have just seen, this rule set prevents both write-up and write-down behavior. (Write-up and write-down apply only to ARRAY security label components and only to write access.) Write-up is when the security label protecting data to which you are attempting to write is higher than the security label you have been granted; write-down is when the security label protecting data is lower.

Which rules are actually used when two security labels are compared is dependent on the type of component used (SET, ARRAY, or TREE) and the type of access being attempted (read or write). Table 7.1 lists the rules found in the DB2LBACRULES rules set, identifies which component each rule is used for, and describes how the rule determines if access is to be blocked.

Table 7.1 Summary of the DB2LBACRULES Rules			
Rule Name Component	Component	Access	Access is blocked when this condition is met
DB2LBACREADARRAY	ARRAY	Read	The user's security label is lower than the protecting security label.
DB2LBACREADSET	SET	Read	There are one or more protecting security labels that the user does not hold.
DB2LBACREADTREE	TREE	Read	None of the user's security labels are equal to or an ancestor of one of the protecting security labels.
DB2LBACWRITEARRAY	ARRAY	Write	The user's security label is higher than the protecting security label or lower than the protecting security label.
DB2LBACWRITESET	SET	Write	There are one or more protecting security labels that the user does not hold.
DB2LBACWRITETREE	TREE	Write	None of the user's security labels are equal to or an ancestor of one of the protecting security labels.
Adapted from Table 78 on pages 608–609 of the *IBM DB2 Version 9 for Linux, UNIX, and Windows Administration Guide—Implementation* manual.			

Granting exemptions

So how can the remaining columns in the EMPLOYEES table be secured with the appropriate security labels? The Security Administrator must first grant user

HR_STAFF an exemption to one or more security policy rules. When a user holds an exemption on a particular security policy rule, that rule is not enforced when the user attempts to access data that is protected by that security policy.

Security policy exemptions are granted by executing the GRANT EXEMPTION ON RULE SQL statement (as a user with SECADM authority). The syntax for this statement is:

```
CREATE EXEMPTION ON RULE [Rule] ,...
FOR [PolicyName]
TO USER [UserName]
```

where:

Rule   Identifies one or more DB2LBACRULES security policy rules for which exemptions are to be given. The following values are valid for this parameter: DB2LBACREADARRAY, DB2LBACREADSET, DB2LBACREADTREE, DB2LBACWRITEARRAY WRITEDOWN, DB2LBACWRITEARRAY WRITEUP, DB2LBACWRITESET, DB2LBACWRITETREE, and ALL. (If an exemption is held for every security policy rule, the user will have complete access to all data protected by that security policy.)

PolicyName   Identifies the security policy for which the exemption is to be granted.

UserName   Identifies the name of the user to which the exemptions specified are to be granted.

Thus, to grant an exemption to the DB2LBACWRITEARRAY rule in the security policy named SEC_POLICY created earlier to a user named HR_STAFF, you would execute a GRANT EXEMPTION statement that looks something like this:

```
GRANT EXEMPTION ON RULE DB2LBACWRITEARRAY
WRITEDOWN FOR sec_policy
TO USER hr_staff
```

Once this exemption is granted along with the appropriate security label, user HR_STAFF will then be able to execute the ALTER TABLE statement shown earlier without generating an error. (Alternately, the following CREATE TABLE statement could be used to create the EMPLOYEES table and protect each column with the appropriate security label, provided user HR_STAFF has the privileges needed to create the table.)

```
CREATE TABLE hr.employees (
        emp_id      INTEGER NOT NULL SECURED WITH confidential,
        f_name      VARCHAR(20) SECURED WITH unclassified,
        l_name      VARCHAR(20) SECURED WITH unclassified,
        gender      CHAR(1) SECURED WITH unclassified,
        hire_date   DATEWITH DEFAULT SECURED WITH classified,
        dept_id     CHAR(5) SECURED WITH unclassified,
        phone       CHAR(14) SECURED WITH unclassified,
        ssn         CHAR(12) SECURED WITH confidential,
        salary      DECIMAL(12,2) SECURED WITH classified,
        bonus       DECIMAL(12,2) SECURED WITH classified)
    SECURITY POLICY sec_policy
```

Putting column-level LBAC into action

Now that we have established a column-level LBAC environment, let's see what happens when different users try to access data stored in protected columns of the EMPLOYEES table. Suppose the user HR_STAFF adds three rows to the EMPLOYEES table by executing the following SQL statements.

```
INSERT INTO hr.employees VALUES(1, 'John', 'Doe', 'M',
    DEFAULT, 'A01', '919-555-1212', '111-22-3333',
    42000.50, 8500.00);

INSERT INTO hr.employees VALUES(2, 'Jane', 'Doe', 'F',
    DEFAULT, 'B02', '919-555-3434', '222-33-4444',
    38000.75, 5000.00);

INSERT INTO hr.employees VALUES(3, 'Paul', 'Smith', 'M',
    DEFAULT, 'C03', '919-555-5656', '333-44-5555',
    39250.00, 3500.00);
```

User HR_STAFF1 has been given read/write access to all columns in the table (with the SEC_POLICY.CLASSIFIED security label and the DB2LBACWRITEARRAY WRITEDOWN exemption), so the statements execute successfully. If user HR_STAFF attempts to query the table, he or she will be able to see every column and every row because he or she has been granted the highest security level in the array.

Now, when user MANAGER1 attempts to read every column in the table, an error will be generated stating that he or she does not have "READ" access to the column "SSN." However, MANAGER1 will be able to execute the following query because he or she has been granted read access to each column specified:

```
SELECT f_name, l_name, hire_date, salary, bonus
FROM hr.employees
```

Now, if user EMPLOYEE1 attempts to execute the same query, an error will be generated stating that he or she does not have "READ" access to the column BONUS. But an attempt by EMPLOYEE1 to execute the following query will be successful:

```
SELECT f_name, l_name, gender, dept_id, phone
FROM hr.employees
```

Additionally, if user MANAGER1 or user EMPLOYEE1 attempt to insert additional records or update existing information, they will get an error stating they do not have permission to perform the operation against the table.

Combining Row-Level and Column-Level LBAC

There may be times when you would like to limit an individual user's access to a specific combination of rows and columns. When this is the case, you must include a column with the data type DB2SECURITYLABEL in the table's definition, add the SECURED WITH [*SecurityLabel*] option to each column in the table's definition, and associate a security policy with the table using the SECURITY POLICY clause of the CREATE TABLE SQL statement or the ADD SECURITY POLICY clause of the ALTER TABLE statement. Typically, you will also create two security label components— one for rows and one for columns—and use both components to construct the security policy and labels needed.

For example, assume that you created two security label components by executing the following commands:

```
CREATE SECURITY LABEL COMPONENT scom_level
ARRAY ['CONFIDENTIAL', 'CLASSIFIED', 'UNCLASSIFIED'];

CREATE SECURITY LABEL COMPONENT scom_country
TREE ('NA' ROOT, 'CANADA' UNDER 'NA', 'USA' UNDER 'NA');
```

You would then create a security policy by executing a CREATE SECURITY POLICY command that looks something like this:

```
CREATE SECURITY POLICY sec_policy
COMPONENTS scom_level, scom_country
WITH DB2LBACRULES
```

Then you could create corresponding security labels by executing commands that look something like this:

```
CREATE SECURITY LABEL sec_policy.confidential
COMPONENT scom_level 'CONFIDENTIAL';

CREATE SECURITY LABEL sec_policy.uc_canada
COMPONENT scom_level 'UNCLASSIFIED'

COMPONENT scom_country 'CANADA';
CREATE SECURITY LABEL sec_policy.uc_us

COMPONENT scom_level 'UNCLASSIFIED'
COMPONENT scom_country 'USA';
```

Finally, after associating the appropriate security labels with individual columns, you would grant the proper security label to each user and conduct a few tests to ensure data access is controlled as expected.

Practice Questions

Question 1

Which of the following is NOT an authentication type that was introduced with DB2 9?

○ A. DATA_ENCRYPT

○ B. DATA_ENCRYPT_KRB

○ C. GSSPLUGIN

○ D. GSS_SERVER_ENCRYPT

Question 2

Which authentication type indicates that authentication occurs at the server workstation, using a Generic Security Service Application Program Interface plug-in?

○ A. GSSPLUGIN

○ B. GSSPLUGINAPI

○ C. GSS_SERVER_ENCRYPT

○ D. GSSAPI_PLUGIN

Question 3

Which of the following authentication types can be used to encrypt XQuery expressions as they are passed between a client and a server?

○ A. CLIENT_ENCRYPT

○ B. SERVER_ENCRYPT

○ C. DATA_ENCRYPT

○ D. KERBEROS

Question 4

Which of the following is NOT a true statement about the GSS_SERVER_ENCRYPT authentication type?

○ A. Authentication occurs at the server workstation, using either the GSSPLUGIN or the SERVER_ENCRYPT authentication method.

○ B. If client authentication occurs through a GSS-API plug-in, the client is authenticated using the first client-supported plug-in found in the list of server-supported plug-ins.

○ C. Authentication occurs at the client workstation, using either the GSSPLUGIN or the CLIENT authentication method.

○ D. If client authentication occurs through a GSS-API plug-in and the client does not support any of the plug-ins found in the server-supported plug-in list, the client is authenticated using the KERBEROS authentication method.

Question 5

Which of the following is NOT used to limit access to individual rows in a table that is protected by Label-Based Access Control (LBAC)?

○ A. One or more security profiles

○ B. A security policy

○ C. One or more security labels

○ D. A DB2SECURITYLABEL column

Question 6

Which of the following best describes what the SECLABEL_TO_CHAR() function is used for?

○ A. To display the security label that has been assigned to a row in an LBAC-protected table.

○ B. To insert a named security label into a DB2SECURITYLABEL column.

○ C. To insert a security label with given component values into a DB2SECURITYLABEL column without having to create a named security label.

○ D. To convert a string to a security label value that has a data type of DB2SECURITYLABEL.

Question 7

Which of the following statements is NOT true about Label-Based Access Control (LBAC)?

○ A. LBAC can be used to restrict access to individual rows and columns in a table or view.

○ B. Users that have been granted different LBAC security labels will get different results when they execute the same query.

○ C. Only users with SYSADM or SECADM authority are allowed to create security policies and security labels.

○ D. Security label components represent criteria that may be used to decide whether a user should have access to specific data.

Question 8

Which of the following SQL statements allows a user named USER1 to write to LBAC-protected columns that have been secured with a LBAC label that indicates a lower level of security than that held by USER1?

○ A. GRANT EXECPTION ON RULE DB2LBACWRITEARRAY WRITEDOWN FOR SEC_POLICY TO USER USER1

○ B. GRANT EXEMPTION ON RULE DB2LBACWRITEARRAY WRITEDOWN FOR SEC_POLICY TO USER USER1

○ C. GRANT EXECPTION ON RULE DB2LBACWRITEARRAY WRITEUP FOR SEC_POLICY TO USER USER1

○ D. GRANT EXEMPTION ON RULE DB2LBACWRITEARRAY WRITEUP FOR SEC_POLICY TO USER USER1

Answers

Question 1

The correct answer is **B**. The following new authentication types were introduced with DB2 9: DATA_ENCRYPT, DATA_ENCRYPT_CMP, GSSPLUGIN, and GSS_SERVER_ENCRYPT.

Question 2

The correct answer is **A**. When the GSSPLUGIN authentication type is used, authentication occurs at the server workstation, using a Generic Security Service Application Program Interface (GSS-API) plug-in. If the client's authentication type is not specified, the server returns a list of server-supported plug-ins (found in the srvcon_gssplugin_list database

manager configuration parameter) to the client. The client then selects the first plug-in found in the client plug-in directory from the list. If the client does not support any plug-in in the list, the client is authenticated using the KERBEROS authentication method.

Question 3

The correct answer is **C**. When the DATA_ENCRYPT authentication type is used, authentication occurs at the server workstation, using the SERVER_ENCRYPT authentication method. In addition, the following data is encrypted before it is passed from client to server and from server to client:

- SQL and XQuery statements.

- SQL program variable data.

- Output data from the server processing of an SQL or XQuery statement and including a description of the data.

- Some or all of the answer set data resulting from a query.

- Large object (LOB) data streaming.

- SQLDA descriptors.

Question 4

The correct answer is **C**. When the GSS_SERVER_ENCRYPT authentication type is used, authentication occurs at the server workstation, using either the GSSPLUGIN or the SERVER_ENCRYPT authentication method. That is, if client authentication occurs through a GSS-API plug-in, the client is authenticated using the first client-supported plug-in found in the list of server-supported plug-ins. If the client does not support any of the plug-ins found in the server-supported plug-in list, the client is authenticated using the KERBEROS authentication method. If the client does not support the Kerberos security protocol, the client is authenticated using the SERVER_ENCRYPT authentication method.

Question 5

The correct answer is **A**. To restrict access to rows in a table using Label-Based Access Control (LBAC), you must define a security label component, define a security policy, create one or more security labels, create an LBAC-protected table or alter an existing table to add LBAC protection (this is done by adding the security policy to the table and defining a column that has the DB2SECURITYLABEL data type), and grant the proper security labels to the appropriate users. There are no LBAC security profiles.

Question 6

The correct answer is **A**. If you want the values of columns with a data type of DB2SECURITYLABEL to be displayed or exported in a human-readable form, you can use the SECLABEL_TO_CHAR() scalar function in a SELECT statement to convert the values to the security label string format.

Question 7

The correct answer is **C**. Security Administrator (SECADM) authority is a special database level of authority that is designed to allow special users to configure various label-based access control (LBAC) elements to restrict access to one or more tables that contain data to which they most likely do not have access themselves. Users with Security Administrator authority are only allowed to perform the following tasks:

- Create and drop security policies.

- Create and drop security labels.

- Grant and revoke security labels to/from individual users (using the GRANT SECURITY LABEL and REVOKE SECURITY LABEL SQL statements).

- Grant and revoke LBAC rule exemptions.

- Grant and revoke SETSESSIONUSER privileges (using the GRANT SETSESSIONUSER SQL statement).

- Transfer ownership of any object not owned by the Security Administrator (by executing the TRANSFER OWNERSHIP SQL statement).

No other authority provides a user with these abilities, including System Administrator authority.

Question 8

The correct answer is **B**. When a user holds an exemption on an LBAC security policy rule, that rule is not enforced when the user attempts to read and/or write data that is protected by that security policy.

Security policy exemptions are granted by executing the GRANT EXEMPTION ON RULE SQL statement (as a user with SECADM authority). The syntax for this statement is:

```
CREATE EXEMPTION ON RULE [Rule] ,...
FOR [PolicyName]
TO USER [UserName]
```

where:

Rule   Identifies one or more DB2LBACRULES security policy rules that exemptions are to be given for. The following values are valid for this parameter: DB2LBACREADARRAY, DB2LBACREADSET, DB2LBACREADTREE, DB2LBACWRITEARRAY WRITEDOWN, DB2LBACWRITEARRAY WRITEUP, DB2LBACWRITESET, DB2LBACWRITETREE, and ALL. (If an exemption is held for every security policy rule, the user will have complete access to all data protected by that security policy.)

PolicyName   Identifies the security policy for which the exemption is to be granted.

UserName   Identifies the name of the user to which the exemptions specified are to be granted.

Thus, to grant an exemption to the DB2LBACWRITEARRAY rule in a security policy named SEC_POLICY to a user named USER1, you would execute a GRANT EXEMPTION statement that looks something like this:

```
GRANT EXEMPTION ON RULE DB2LBACWRITEARRAY
WRITEDOWN FOR sec_policy
TO USER user1
```

Index

NOTE: Boldface numbers indicate illustrations; t indicates a table

More DB2 Books from MC Press

DB2 9 Fundamentals Certification Study Guide
ISBN: 978-158347-072-5
Author: Roger E. Sanders
http://www.mc-store.com/5088

DB2 9 Linux, UNIX, and Windows Database Adminstrator Certification Study Guide
ISBN: 978-158347-077-8
Author: Roger E. Sanders
http://www.mc-store.com/5090

DB2 9 for z/OS Database Adminstrator Certification Study Guide
ISBN: 978-158347-074-9
Authors: Susan Lawson and Dan Luksetich
http://www.mc-store.com/5089
Available: November 2007

DB2 9 for Linux, UNIX, and Windows Advanced Database Administrator Certification Study Guide
ISBN: 978-158347-080-0
Authors: Roger Sanders and Dwaine Snow
http://www.mc-store.com/5093
Available: May 2008

DB2 9 for Developers
ISBN: 978-158347-071-8
Author: Philip K. Gunning
http://www.mc-store.com/5086
Available: January 2008